THIRSTY
FOR
CHANGE

DEDICATION

This book is dedicated to my loving wife Denise and our growing family of eighteen along with the special people of *Crown Christian Church*. Thank you for partnering in the creation and development of the *FBJ Kingdom* Cultural Leadership Center. Together we [continue to] change lives globally!

To every aspiring leader, even those who find life too busy, aimlessly empty, and ineffective ...

To you, the reader—I desire for you *a purposed-driven life* characterized by effectiveness, efficiency, and personal fulfillment.

To all who may be oppressed by the ignorance of leaders who malpractice …

To every generation seeking meaningful reasons to live, learn, and ultimately lead …

To every committed leader and individual seeking these tools for himself …

This work is dedicated to you!

Unless otherwise noted, Scripture quotations are taken from the KING JAMES VERSION (*KJV*) of the Holy Bible. Amplified quotations are indicated as (*AMP*). New Living Translation quotations are indicated as (*NLT*). All versions used by permission of the copyright owners.

Published in South Carolina by:
FBush Publishing
P.O. Box 7690 N
Augusta, S.C. 29861
Web address: www.FBJM.org
Email: FBushPublishing@gmail.com
In conjunction with *Carsamonte Publishing*
(CarsamontePublishing@gmail.com)

Editorial and publishing:
First-line and developmental editing: Carmen Glover, CarsamontePublishing@gmail.com
Proofing: Carmen Glover
Cover and interior Design by: Your Vision Told.
Reviews by: Carmen Glover
Thirsty for Change: A Guide to Balanced Leading was printed in the United States of America.
ISBN 978-0-9990941-0-5

TABLE OF CONTENTS

WHAT OTHERS ARE SAYING ABOUT
THIRSTY FOR CHANGE!

"ONE OF THE HARDEST THINGS FOR A GOOD LEADER TO FIND IS another great leader to pour into and pull out of them. Dr. Bush has a keen and unique ability to identify the greatness and potential of a leader. At the same time, he identifies the frailties of their humanity. The fruit of personal development is the overflow to those who follow. Get connected to this great leader if you're ready to transcend the level you're currently on!"

LaChish J. Latimer, Captain,
U.S. Army Nurse Corp; RN, BSN, MSN

———————❖———————

A LEADER AMONG MEN!
"Bishop Finace Bush Jr. is a man who regularly seeks the presence of God through prayer and close communion. Enoch, Noah, and Abraham knew God closely; as friend-to-friend. There is a vast difference between knowledge 'of God' and knowing God personally. There is a huge difference between a religious man who holds true to all sorts of rules

and rituals, and a man who walks closely with the living God. Bishop Bush is on a step-by-step friendship journey with God!"

CALVIN PADGETT, PHD,
Teacher McCormick High School –
Business Education, Strayer University School of Business
(Adjunct)

❖

❝DR. FINACE BUSH JR. IS A MASTERFUL TEACHER ON THE PRINCIPLES of leadership. His teaching style captivates, motivates, and challenges students to press beyond mediocrity and excel for the Kingdom of God. Dr. Bush models the intricate 'balance' of effective leadership responsibilities. This is essential for today's Kingdom leaders and Dr. Bush is committed to advancing the Kingdom of God. His strategic approach develops and empowers leaders in the making. It's time for the body of Christ to move forward, Thirsty for Change, is the drink we desperately need!"

BISHOP SOLOMON SMITH
Mount Moriah Christian Center
Waukegan, IL

❖

❝BISHOP BUSH IS A WONDERFUL MAN OF GOD AND A NATURAL leader's Leader. His wisdom and deep faith are an inspiration to anyone fortunate enough to be in his company. He is highly energetic and a vibrant leader. It is an honor to call him not just 'friend,' but a 'dear friend' and a moral leader by example.❞

JOHN CAPES, CCIM

❝BISHOP FINACE BUSH JR. IS A VOICE OF DEVELOPMENT AND training for this particular generation. My personal life and ministry has been sharpened and challenged by the insight and passion of Dr. Bush. His ability to articulate the mind of God is impeccable. He has taken time to personally walk me through the process of development. Bishop Bush's teachings and writings are a blessing to the wholeness of mankind.❞

PASTOR DANIEL LATIMER

❝A PIONEER IN CHRISTIAN LEADERSHIP AND DEVELOPMENT, DR. Finace Bush Jr. is an astute, anointed, effective, powerful, and captivating teacher. His teachings are relevant, cross-generational, doctrinally sound, and most of all; life transforming.

I am honored to have Dr. Bush as a spiritual father and trusted mentor for more than twenty years. While under his leadership I have experienced growth and prospered in ways beyond my most vivid imaginations. Today, I am a grateful, humbled and proud licensed minister, published author, corporate trainer, a business owner and Certified Personal- and Christian-life coach.

'Give a man a fish, you'll feed him for a day. Teach a man to fish and you'll feed him for a lifetime.

-Chinese Proverb'"

CYNTHIA A. GOLSON STEEL
CEO iSpeakLife Corp.
North Augusta, SC

❖

INTRODUCTION

I thirst ...

Imagine yourself as a leader in a desert; a dry place with hardly any cover. It's hot, intensely penetrating, and humid. You shift, but keep moving your team forward. This rapidly escalating heat is mobile and transitional. It's tailored to fit you like a garment. It actually wears you better than the seasonal garments you thought would suffice in this place.

In previous stretches and other assignments, you've contended with heat, but never to this magnitude and never for this length of time. Adjusting to each of your physical features and every square inch of your charred body, this heat gradually becomes unrelenting. You begin removing layers of garments you once thought were necessary and definitely appropriate for your journey.

The parched torn ground you traveled to get to this place is without compassion or compromise, not yielding any sign of moisture to indicate or even hint that water is located anywhere in this vicinity. As time transpires, the reality is setting in that if something doesn't happen soon, the stay and duration of the drought will have stimulated new illusions and rationales that diametrically oppose your purpose for being in this region.

Deep anguish, and the feeling of agonizing despair under the constant offensive, multidimensional and multidirectional, adversarial climate makes you realize just

11

how isolated and alone you are in this place. Suddenly, after long deliberation, questioning how you got here, your vision now marred with mirages forces you to howl and wail from within as you lament, *"Father, if you are willing, let this bitter cup be passed from me?"* Or, *"Lord, do you really care that we are perishing?"*

In recognition of your own emptiness, inability, and inadequacies, you finally quiet yourself within, as you now begin to internalize your struggle. Realizing in the quietness of the late evening that you are here on assignment, you have an epiphany, which lets you know that your purpose and destiny extends far beyond this deserted place. In fact, even though you naturally feel you're being suffocated and crucified on a cross, you begin *counting it all joy!* Glorying in your afflictions and tribulations, knowing that the next phase of your journey is near.

Through the joy initiated by your praise, an internal glimpse of an image that was dormant in your spirit, from a promise about your purpose, became the catalyst that pushed you to pray the most empathic, proficient and relevant prayer during your greatest moment of transition and change; *Lord, "I thirst!"*

Two words that when combined together personalizes the willingness and readiness of an individual to transition towards the fulfillment of the next phase of their destiny. Thirst, a sentiment of the soul that expresses the times and need for change. *"I thirst"* personalizes the individuals need from a particular resource to cool their soul's interest in order to properly hydrate for what's next in line. In this case its spiritual righteousness and it can only be filled by the Sovereign Deity, who created us and left this void within us because, only He is responsible for our existence.

Picture Noah after one hundred years removed from his visitation to build an ark, still waiting for God's return. *Abraham* nearly twenty-five years removed from the promise when the *Lord* appeared to him by the terebinth trees of Mamre as he sat in the tent's door, in the heat of the day. Lifting up his eyes he looked, and behold, three men stood by him; when he saw them, he ran from the tent to meet them, and bowed himself to the ground, and said, *"My Lord, if I have now found favor in Your sight, do not pass on by Your servant."* Picture *Isaac* in a severe famine, preparing to flee south to Egypt when the *Lord* appeared to him and said: *"Do not go down to Egypt; live in the land of which I shall tell you." Jacob*, who sent presents over to Esau before him, but he, himself, lodged that night in the camp. When he was left alone, *"…a Man wrestled with him until the breaking of day."* Picture *Joseph*, rejected by his brothers, who went from pit, to prison, to palace. As he died, made mention of the departure of the children of Israel, and gave instructions concerning his bones."

Picture *Moses* eighty years into his destiny as he tended the flock of Jethro, his father-in-law, he came to the back of the desert; Horeb, the *mountain of God*. An angel of the *Lord* appeared to him in a flame of fire from the midst of a bush. So he looked, and behold, the bush burned with fire, but it was not consumed. Then Moses said, *"I will now turn aside and see this great sight, why the bush does not burn."* Many others throughout both Testaments have also demonstrated the power of a *thirsty soul.*

John 19:28-30 says, *"Jesus, knowing that all things were now accomplished, that the Scripture might be fulfilled, said, I thirst!"*

As children of God, we should never take on battles under the power of our own strength. Only in recognition of our own emptiness do we mourn our own unrighteousness while submitting our power to God. With righteousness, once our thirst is quenched, that thirst for righteousness continually grows. We should keep fueling that desire to satisfy our lives with it at every phase of our course.

Matthew 5:6 is a powerful passage, because it exudes hope: *"Blessed are those who hunger and thirst after righteousness for they shall be filled."*

Here it emphatically states that we *are* blessed *if* we hunger and thirst after righteousness. Why are we blessed, "if"? Because we are filled! Or, as indicated in the promise, *we shall be filled.* In this Jesus, Himself assures us that our satisfaction has already been met in Him, even in drought and famine. Everything we need to fulfill our purpose for being, doing, and having is unlocked by these two words combined together *I thirst!*

We may define our physiological and safety needs as *having needs*. Our belonging and self-esteem as *doing needs*, and self-actualization as our *being needs*. Since Apostle Paul said, "in Christ" we have our being, it is safe to conclude that our quest to self-discovery and purpose should begin with an insatiable and unquenchable thirst for God's righteousness.

Why is hunger and thirst such a good illustration? Because as water and food is to the body, so righteousness is to the spirit. We as human's hunger and thirst, not only for food but for satisfaction in life. We search all kinds of areas to be filled, to be satisfied. But we most often, fall short.

Ecclesiastes 3:11 says, *"He has made everything beautiful in its time. Also He has put eternity in their hearts, except that no one can find out the work that God does from beginning to end."*

John Piper states: *"God has put eternity in our hearts and we have an inconsolable longing."* Blaise Pascal said that we all have a *"God-shaped void"* in our lives. All men hunger and thirst; the problem is that we try to fill them with things other than the righteousness of God. Some reading this book are empty like I once was—*you have not been satisfied.* You try to fill a *"God-shaped void"* in your life with superficial things only to find you are still empty and unsatisfied.

In Isaiah 55:1-2, there is an incredible message of hope for you if you seek the answer. *"Ho! The prophet cries, 'Everyone who thirsts, come to the waters; and you who have no money, come, buy and eat. Yes, come, buy wine and milk without money and without price. Why do you spend money for what is not bread, and your wages for what does not satisfy? Listen carefully to Me, and eat what is good, and let your soul delight itself in abundance."*

Jesus fulfilled everything necessary within the scope of mortality in three and a half years to purchase redemption for all humanity. He was now thirsty for the remaining portion of His purpose, which was to descend into the lower region of hell and lead out those in captivity; giving gifts to men. Even though alone, isolated, and deserted in an exceedingly dry place, He was not afraid, but ready as a corn of wheat to endure the transitions of death.

Note, *"Now a vessel full of sour wine was sitting there; and they filled a sponge with sour wine, put it on hyssop, and put it to His mouth. So when Jesus had received the sour wine, He said, "It is finished!" And bowing His head, He gave up His spirit."*

As kingdom leaders, much of our plight is bittersweet like "sour wine on hyssop" as it is summed up in this metaphor to mirror the constant struggle associated with our assignments. But kingdom leaders who thirst for righteousness is the source of many of the greatest reforms in the historical world. Perhaps most notably the abolition of slavery in Great Britain and the United States and the genesis of the Civil Rights Movement. But again, this beatitude is important because it has been the catalyst in the spirit that prompts the initiative to pursue change.

C.S. Lewis states:

"Being made righteous, according to Paul in his epistle to the Romans, is therefore the fruit of conversion; a real and living change in one's heart and behaviors that results in being united to Christ — being in Christ — and doesn't seem to really have much to do with legal status."

We often allow our basic human need for the grace of God, the presence of divine love, and His righteousness revealed in Jesus Christ, to be fragmented through resistance and rebellion against God. We try, like our first parents, to fill the need without God, to eat the forbidden fruit, to be made wise through our own energy and effort without grace or the presence of divine love. Because of the condition of death in which we live in the fallen cosmos, the fragmented need for God transmutes into a multitude of small hungers, miniscule thirsts, which inform the body's natural appetites beyond their legitimate use.

A misdirected thirst for love (God) might then be

transmuted into sexual lust; a desire to possess another person, as if to fulfill one's need. Or in the insatiable thirst for success, fame, recognition—all symptoms stemming from a desire to be loved, turns into appetites that lead to numbing habits, addictions, and enslavement to one's own body.

Hunger is twisted into avarice, our bellies become our gods and thirsts turns into a type of vampirism. In this, we destroy rather than commune with those we seek to control or coerce in the name of love. Also, we do this in the name of success, profit, or any number of other contemporary ambitions fueled by fragmented needs that have turned into passionate desires. These seems to adhere to the flesh itself and can never be satisfied.

St. John Chrysostom, in elucidating this beatitude says that the opposite of *the virtue of righteousness* is covetousness. This is a driving force in many lives — the desire to have something we do not have, that we see others have. It isn't necessarily limited to material possessions, but can be many other things. Coveting privileges, or fame, or power, or control, or even to be someone we are not.

The person who hungers and thirsts after righteousness recognizes his own poverty and through poverty of spirit has the humility to submit himself to God. In this, this person does not seek to possess a multitude of things or to control other people. Instead, this person possesses the Kingdom of God. Mourning the condition of death and all the consequent separations, he repents and is cleansed of bodily defilement through his own tears. In meekness he does not compete or compare himself with others in a struggle for what is not really needful.

He begins to hunger and thirst, not to satisfy various lusts for pleasure, to numb fear through comforting habits or through pride and shame, but for the righteousness of God to be manifested in Him and through Him as he participates in divine life through faith in Jesus Christ.

Jesus says in the Sermon on the Mount that he will be filled, which we may take to mean that He will become righteous. "*Thirst*" is specific, it's directional, it's a connector, a great motivator, a signal of void or emptiness and special need, a distinguisher of a particular craving or need. A sign of hope; our hope for *righteousness* is how we are saved.

To hunger and thirst is continual. Every day is a pattern repeated in each of us, because our bodies have need of food and water. This is the same in the spiritual realm of life. In these passages, the psalmist is clear on what it means to long, hunger, and thirst for righteousness. "*Early will I seek You; My soul thirsts for You; My flesh longs for You.*" "*As the deer pants for the water brooks, so pants my soul for You, O God.*"

Do you have this longing, this passion, this unquenchable thirst for righteousness? Is this something you cannot live without? This is what we, as Believers, should thirst for. We need to hunger and thirst after God on a daily basis; every second of every day. So much so, that we cannot live without satisfying it. We think many things we do in our lives will not affect our relationship with Christ, but it does.

What things do your heart long for? What things
do your heart thirst for? Is it as Paul says, *"That I
may know Him and the power of His resurrection"?*
(Philippians 3:10)

Hunger and thirsting for righteousness has both an evangelistic message for those who don't know Christ, as well as a message for those in Christ. Within these pages, I've outlined several objects of kingdom leadership. First, to provide the foundational stones to kingdom leadership and I conclude with a simple question: *What do you hunger and thirst for in your life?* I pray that we, as kingdom citizens and leaders, can honestly answer; *"righteousness."*

The eternal question is: What makes a good leader? What attributes and objects do successful leaders have in common? Although there may be no definitive answer, there is but one certainty. As business technologies, ministries, and processes evolve and employee demographics shift, the best leaders are those who change with the times. They have both foresight and adaptability. The new trend is to customize a specific culture within an organization, its mission, and the personality of its workforce rather than rule solely from a manual.

This book was written to sustain the ministers, leaders, and their families in the midst of gruesome exchanges and laborious trials as they sacrifice daily to lead God's people and society.

A Kingdom assignment is an induction into a journey

filled with unpredictables, uncertainties, and variables which are independent, dependent, and controlled. It is also a life of constant warfare and indifference. Meaning, the Kingdom is always under assault.

These personal and positional initiatives require wisely guided prudence with untiring alertness if one is to succeed with correct attitudes, postures, and self-control. *"You are sent out as sheep in the midst of wolves. Be wise as serpents and harmless as doves."*

A leader must be conscious of the primary objects to maintain a sense of purpose and focus to overcome pressures of the position. A leader must remain steadfast while enduring positional trials, challenges, and persecutions from indifference.

CHAPTER 1
MY GREAT AWAKENING

It's 4:35 AM and I've been in meditation for the last twenty minutes since finishing intercessory prayer. This morning's devotion was different. I needed God's *peace* as confirmation of what and how much information I could share of my personal experiences. The time is relevant because, for the past thirty-five years of my life, I began my devotion at this time two to five days per week. Doing this allowed me to continually develop my relationship with God. It's probably, the single *key* factor that fortified within me, stability and strength as a leader to withstand many test and trials.

Years ago, I began seeking God in New Ellenton, South Carolina; my place of birth. It was there, as a teenager in Junior High School, that I received my first visitation regarding my call to ministry. It was a rainy Tuesday night. I decided this would be my last day pretending to agree with the Christian Doctrine. A group of young adults and middle-aged men and women moved into our community from Philadelphia. They called themselves the Moorish Vanguards.

They were excellent musicians and played their instruments a couple of hours each evening while cooking well-flavored fish to attract young inquiring minds. After attracting a small crowd, they'd share contrasting insights between the King James Bible and the Quran. They seemed to know much more about the Bible than the Sunday School teachers and deacons at my church. Especially to a young novice mind desiring to know the truth. So, after about three months of visiting with them daily after school, I was convinced that the black man was being deceived by the white man's religion. They convinced me that the Bible was the tool the slave master used to pull it off.

A small group of us were ready to progress to the next phase. It was time to change my name from the slave-masters name to my original name. While I prepared to denounce my old belief and declare my new name in the Nation of Islam, things started falling apart.

My intent was to sneak into the house and talk to my mother while everyone else was gone. I could avoid ridicule and mocking by my siblings or so I thought. However, the rain forced them inside and my father came home from work earlier than expected. I arrived home from the meeting, headed for the den, and noticed my mother ironing and talking with dad. Everyone else watched TV, laughing, and talking. Suddenly, I became frustrated and stormed to my bedroom where I kept all my literature.

As I entered my room, a strange feeling of conviction came over me and I felt sorry for myself. I didn't know if I felt like a family misfit, or if I needed to hear from God before going any further. So, I snatched my Bible from the nightstand and threw it across the floor and wept. I fell to my knees beside the bed and cried. Vehemently, I shouted, "God if you're *real*, I need to know *right now* or don't ever bother me again! Whoever you are!" I said, *"Reveal yourself to me because I don't know what I'm doing and I don't want to be lost. Are you Allah, Jehovah, Elohim, El Emmanuel, JESUS ... who?"*

My brother entered the room, made a sarcastic comment, and swiftly exited. Then dad peeked in and asked, *"Boy, you in here praying this time of day instead of watching TV?"* Not knowing what I was dealing with, he left the door cracked and went down the hall, thank God! As I arose from my knees to turn off the lamp, I noticed the Bible open with one page visible. It was Isaiah 55, verses 6 -11. It was the first time I'd ever seen this chapter. So, I read it several times, *"Seek* ye the Lord *while He* may be found, *call* ye upon him *while He is near*: Let the wicked forsake his way, and the unrighteous man his thoughts: and let him *return* unto the LORD, and he will have mercy upon him; and to our God, for he will abundantly pardon." I read over the highlighted sentences several times before moving forward. Then this next sentence gripped my heart: *"For my thoughts are not your thoughts, neither are your ways my ways, saith the Lord."*

Although I was astonished, I was still determined to not be moved. *"For as the heavens are higher than the earth, so are my ways higher than your ways, and my thoughts than your thoughts. For as the rain cometh down, and the snow from heaven, and returneth not thither, but watereth the earth, and maketh it bring forth and bud, that it may give seed to the sower, and bread to the eater: So shall my word be that goeth forth out of my mouth: it shall not return unto me void, but it shall accomplish that which I please, and it shall prosper in the thing whereto I sent it."* After completing verse eleven, I laid across my bed. Thinking this was sheer coincidence, I tossed it up again to see where it would land this time. To my amazement, it landed exposing the Gospel of John, Chapter One. I read the first twelve verses. But it was verses ten through twelve that demanded my attention. *"He was in the world, and the world was made by Him, and the "world knew Him not."* This is exactly how it looked to me on that dreary, rainy night. *"He came unto his own, and his own received him not. But as many as received him, to them gave he power to become the sons of GOD, even to them that believe on His name."* (*KJV*)

I continued to toss the Bible several more times to see how long this would continue. Romans 8:1-14 and Romans 10:1-15 were also passages that lept from the pages. To this day, I still quote these Scriptures verbatim without intentional practice or rehearsal; solely from memory. Although I prayed and apologized for my disdain and contemptible behavior toward

God and His Word, I sought the *truth* and God came through for me to prevent my collapse. Suddenly, I was on a mission to correctly define God's name and distinguish it from Allah.

My parents were good about buying me biblical literature because I enjoyed them. I simply did not comprehend academics like my siblings. So, I sat on the side of the bed and researched *Names of God* until I fell asleep. Since the first visitation until now, I rely on the Bible as my life-principle. It is my only true life-source, without hesitation.

After the confirming experience, I witnessed throughout my community and the CSRA communities from the age of fourteen to seventeen. I successfully recruited and discipled nearly 170 young converts who ranged in age from fourteen to thirty-six. The majority of us met on Saturday nights until midnight for choir rehearsal, Bible study, and prayer service. Many of these converts are now preachers, pastors, evangelist, teachers, educators, politicians, and civic leaders.

Although I am ready at any time to defend God's truth in context, the Bible is not a source of debate for me. Even though I've made my share of mistakes, fallen into horrible pits, made lots of untimely decisions, which doesn't place me among the wisest of leaders, the *grace* of God still prevails in my life, forty-five years later, this same *grace - life* principle has revealed in me the ability to find my center; my inner core, which makes life easier to discern and prioritize for the sake of godly and personal fulfillment. With this kind of personal peace and inner stability, I'm able to live a well-balanced life of symmetry and stability in spite of circumstances and situations. I've written in detail about it in my book, "*Structure: The Master Key to Kingdom Success.*"

Matthew Henry said, "*We mistake our religion if we look upon it only as a system of notions and a guide to speculation. No, it is a practical religion that tends to the right ordering of the conversation. It is designed not only to inform our judgments, but to reform our hearts and lives.*"

The Kingdom leader must know that Life has *issues*. Not singular, but plural. We cannot focus all our attention on one aspect of life and expect to be whole and complete. These issues range from personal, marriage, family, relations, spiritual, emotional, mental, educational, financial, food, health, eating, thinking, shelter, behavior, occupation, duties, responsibilities, obligation, commitment, etc. These issues and more must be championed if we're to experience a consistent, wholesome, and fulfilled life.

CHAPTER 2
MY CALL TO MINISTRY

In the eleventh grade, I was awarded a scholarship to the University of Kansas. I left home for college on June 7, 1978. After attending the University of Kansas for one-quarter, I decided to transfer to AIA in Atlanta, Georgia to be closer to home. During this time, I explored and experimented with alcohol attempting to fit in with my roommates and school peers. Hoping to convince God that I was not fit to preach the gospel any longer, I developed a habit of casual drinking and partying on weekends. No matter how hard I tried to separate myself from my former life, situations would occur among my peers that demanded my spiritual insight or *Christ-like* compassion to manifest. These situations and circumstances would range from providing food to directing relationships or simply assisting with personal-life issues.

One Thursday evening, after a long week of school we prepared for the next week's final exams. I decided to turn in early, pack for a weekend trip home, and watch television with one of my roommates. We sat in the living room laughing and sipping a little Tequila Sunrise. I consumed about four ounces when I was suddenly convicted about drinking. I mentioned it to my roommate, who suggested that even though he was comfortable with it, casual drinking never seemed to fit my personality. He pointed out that other students often considered me to be above certain behaviors because they looked to me for leadership in many areas.

That night, became the beginning of the end of my college career as a student endeavoring to become a professional artist. Around eleven o'clock that night, we both decided to turn in for the night. But little did I know, I was in for a visitation that would literally change the course and direction of my life forever.

As I entered the bedroom it seemed like someone or some presence was already there. After showering and preparing for bed, I noticed my roommate had gone out to discard the trash never made it back to his bed. So, I got into my bed located on the other side of the room and pulled the covers over my head since I left the light on for my roommate.

Suddenly, as I attempted to rest, I heard a voice say, *"Finace, Finace, turn over."* Thinking it might have been my roommate, I gradually turned and pulled the covers from over my head and there it was. The brightest, most attractive, and brilliantly glowing light I had ever seen. From out of this impressively beautiful, majestically glorious, and brilliantly breathtaking light came a voice that first said, *"Your roommate will not be coming to bed tonight."* Wondering if I was dreaming, He said: *"I have come to tell you it is time for you to return home and become a witness for Me in the community you were raised in."* I thought, 'Wow!' I must have drank more than I realized. But the voice insisted. *"You do not need to worry about finals tomorrow because there will be none. You are to prepare to leave school tomorrow and return home. Tell only your mother and a senior mother in the community whom I've prepared to receive you. Others will not understand, so don't mention it to them until I have established you without their assistance."*

As I lay there looking into this light and listening to this calming and assuring voice, I asked. *"Who will pay the remaining balance of my school tuition and fees? Because if this is you, Lord I do not want any more financial assistance from my parents, they will not understand me leaving without finishing the last quarter to get my degree."* He kindly said, *"I have provided for you."* The rest of the conversation was very detailed and directional, and I listened intently until I fell asleep.

I had *never* experienced such peace and wholesomeness in my life. This visitation was like nothing I'd ever imagined. It is the ultimate culmination of all my best natural and spiritual experiences combined.

The next morning as I prepared for school, heading down the stairs I noticed my roommate lying on the couch asleep. So I woke him and asked why he never came to his bed. He said, once he took out the trash and put his leftovers away, a strong fatigue and tiredness came over him and made it too difficult for him to climb the stairs.

He said it was so overwhelming that all he could do was lay on the couch until he went to sleep.

I sat briefly to share my experience with him. While going through the details I stopped and said, *"In fact, the voice said don't worry about finals nor school today."* He sat in awe, listening as I listed the instructions and details involved that needed to be confirmed. Finally, I decided to wait for him as he hurried to prepare for school.

Leaving the apartment, we noticed students from the 8:30 a.m. classes returning early from school. They were all waving and trying to get our attention, to let us know that school was closed that day due to mechanical problems and there were no finals.

My roommate suddenly stopped, firmly stared at me, and said, *"Well, there it is, it's begun already. Looks like God intends to get your attention for sure! Wow, man that's awesome,"*

After putting our school supplies in the apartment, we went to the Southern Bell office on Buford Highway to check on our telephone situation at the apartment. As we entered, there were about six lines, all full, waiting to be served. We took turns standing in line until we made it to a representative. My roommate suggested I grab the vacant seat near the phone service while he took the first turn. Following his suggestion, I made my way to a swiveling chair and spun around. I looked down and noticed five, that's right "5" brand new, crisp, one-hundred dollar bills on the floor beneath my chair.

I reached down and picked them up off the floor and headed towards the counter to see if anyone present was missing $500. Pressed as if they were freshly warmed from the printer's mint, I noticed each bill felt brand new. After consulting with my roommate, who initially thought I should keep it a secret. We determined it would have been tragic for either of us to be missing $500 at that time. I spoke with the supervisor who instructed me to keep the money over the weekend to see if anyone came in to inquire about it. A week passed without any inquiries. This was my second major encounter.

On Monday the following week, after returning to Atlanta I decided to go back to school and finish my finals. While in class I was handed a note from the finance department requesting I visit the administrator. As I entered the room upstairs, it appeared she had been waiting for me. I sat in the chair in front of her desk, and she firmly asked, "*Are you Finace Bush?*" Yes, I replied. Immediately she began calling out delinquent quarterly fees with seemingly, an angry tone. While I was listening cautiously my mind shifted to the conversation I had earlier with the voice during my visitation. After she finished I silently stood a little intimidated and headed for the door. Nearing the exit, I heard her shout in anguish as she yelled my name. "*Finace, Mr. Bush, I'm sorry!*" "*I just realized in my stack of papers under the past due fees are the checks from various entities and organizations that have come in and they more than payout your fees."*

She began, *"A check from.... sent $14,000. Here's another check from...., and another from...and another, and another,"* until I literally left the office with *all* of my debts paid and $1400 to put in my pocket!

I called home to share my new miracle with mom and she said: *"Well, if you think you need to come back home, go ahead and get everything packed to leave Friday."* I later learned that Mom had been dreaming about my visitations but didn't understand what they meant. She later stated, *"I knew God was trying to tell me something about your calling because these were the same dreams I had while carrying you nine months."*

After returning home I received –two-to-three checks in the mail in increments of $150 - $400 for the next three weeks until the second week after I was hired at the textile mill as a porter.

The Holy Spirit continued to direct me by that same voice. I would witness daily and lead many souls to Christ. My devotional periods each morning around 4:30 am became very exciting experiences and informative encounters that would generate a spiritual boldness like nothing I'd ever known. Every step was ordered so definitively that it was easy to confirm God's leading and see evidential manifestations and results.

On Friday and Saturday nights, I would witness at the neighborhood clubs and taverns during parties and bingo events. The discotheque owner, Mr. N. Bing once asked me to please slow down visits during his parties because it was having a significant economic impact. One night I took a small group of new converts into the cotton club during bingo and I was greeted by church deacons, trustees, and ushers who suddenly began tipping out with their finger raised, attempting to exit silently. This prompted a tremendous amount of resistance throughout the church community among leaders.

We experienced many new converts, miraculous encounters, and confirmable healing manifestations each week. I was led to start a Saturday Night Prayer Meeting which grew into a large Bible study that averaged –sixty-to-ninety participants between ages of fourteen and thirty-six every weekend in my parents' backyard. These were powerful and highly-anointed meetings that attracted multitudes of young men and women from throughout the CSRA community.

Mother B. Paige, a well-known community leader, contacted me and an influential young lady in the Aiken area, Gina, about starting a community choir which became the Aiken Community Choir. The young group became the inspiration for many teens and young adults and headlined on average, up to six programs weekly. Excited during every occasion, our practices turned into anointed services and empowering experiences that gained a tremendous amount of attention among community and church leaders. Eventually, the adversary prompted some crooked, under-cover religious leaders who started looking for ways to shut us down, even though their very sons and daughters were among the fellowship.

One night during prayer service, the Holy Spirit overshadowed the entire group as we begin praying in the spirit, speaking in tongues and prophesying. Many souls were added to Heaven's roster that night.

Around 1:30 a.m. that Sunday morning, we were still gathered when the Holy Spirit revealed to me that Freddie Roundtree would come out of a comma at 5:30 a.m. I prophesied it to the group. He led me to have my sister call two women who were related to Freddie Roundtree as he lay in a coma six months after a traumatic car accident which left him severely injured from head-to-toe.

I will never forget this experience because when I arrived on the scene of the actual accident six months earlier. I was led to put my hand on his head and begin to pray as the paramedics and fire team entered the site. While checking his vitals, the medic said to me, *"Young man I don't know what you're doing, but stay right here and keep doing it because it's keeping him alive. Really he should already be dead!"*

The scene was bloody and the jaws of life were used to cut him out of the car. His skull was crushed, leaving his brain exposed. His face severely fractured, torso severed in two, spine broken, pelvic crushed, leaving his intestines exposed from his side. His legs and hips were also broken and each breath seemed as if it were his last. I prayed fervently in the Spirit and he fought hard for every breath. I continued to pray and my hand stayed on his head until he was given oxygen and fully fastened to his bed for transport.

Several times during that morning the team of doctors shared that the family should begin preparing for his death. But he pulled through by the Grace of God. After his first couple of weeks in intensive care, he lay in a full body cast nearly two months. Over the next few months, they did a series of surgeries until gradually they exposed his repaired wounds.

Immediately, my sister Rhonda coordinated how they would arrive and they all obeyed the instructions the Holy Spirit had given me. Entering his room, they gathered around Freddie's bedside that morning to witness him awake from the lengthy coma.

I remember several occasions wherein the doctors summoned the family together fearing he wouldn't overcome all the injuries and some of the infections and challenges that would arise. But this particular day would yield a notable miracle unlike anything we'd ever heard of in our community. At 5:30 AM Freddie awakened from the coma trying to free himself as if he were running frantically from someone trying to subdue him. He later testified that two dreadful-looking creatures that he first thought were Angels until they clutched each of his arms, were given permission to escort him to the dreadful region of hell. Approaching the hot, slimy, awful and fiery site, he started crying out for another chance and kicking as he yelled my name.

We were in high praise during worship service all day in each of the churches we visited. Sharing the good news prompted many of his family and friends, along with many others to receive Christ as their savior. Of course, the enemy was also stirred. Opposition began to surface when after another healing miracle featuring a senior mother in the community, I was called to a meeting and instructed along with several others to stop having prayer meetings and influencing these young people to give up their opportunity to be young and enjoy their lives.

They emphatically told me, *"You'd better go enjoy your youth and sow your wild oats because you only live once."* But they couldn't understand that my daily joy and excitement was witnessing the lives that were changing throughout our community. This was *life* to me! By now, I was approaching twenty and was sure this was God's will for my life. I was studious, courageous, strong-willed, and radical. Although I made many mistakes as a leader while violating church order and protocol that didn't align with Scripture. I sincerely looked for a spiritual guide that would direct me in my new life.

I also knew I needed discipline because suddenly, *my good was being evil spoken of.* I was constantly being misunderstood while helping church leaders that demonstrated a lack of godliness and righteous behaviors. As a young firm believer of truth, I actually thought it was my responsibility to correct everything and everyone that held the position of a church leader but reflected the opposite. I never intended to make so many enemies, but I did.

Even though I was constantly sought after as a songster

and speaker along with my choirs, I became revered by my local contemporaries as a radical who interfered with normal traditional services. I was also accused of teaching doctrines that represented Pentecost, Apostolic, and Holiness denominations. I'm also reminded of another easily confirmable miracle that took place at the Medical College of Georgia located in Augusta, which was witnessed by others. One day while out witnessing, I received a call that my choir secretary, Mrs. Joann Lewis, was rushed to the hospital threatening a miscarriage. After receiving the message, I took one of my partners with me to visit with her. Upon entering the hospital, I was notified that she had a very traumatic miscarriage and the nursing staff had completed her DNC.

Undaunted by the report, a spirit of boldness came upon me immediately. I scanned the waiting room and realized everyone had given up. Even one of my spiritual mentors who had become a sponsorship host for our prayer meetings on Saturday nights. Suddenly, the Holy Spirit spoke to me and said: *"Take her husband with you to see her and anoint her while speaking these words to her."* As I obeyed, the resistance from her family and friends in the room mounted and became very obvious. Turning away from the doubters, I clutched Sonny's hand and said: *"Let's go to her room."*

The Holy Spirit said, *"Take me to her room!"* As we entered the room the head nurse instructed me to be brief. Joann replied, *"He's my minister, it's ok."* Her husband held my hand firmly as I took out my anointing oil and began anointing her head.

Standing by her bedside, I said to her with a stern voice. *"You shall not lose your child, says the Lord!"* Their eyes stretched as I continued, *"You will give birth to a healthy little girl."* Immediately, Sonny, her husband replied. *"But the doctor said the miscarriage was totally finished and the x-rays confirmed that her womb is totally cleansed and the nurses have completed her DNC."* I asked if she believed that God sent me to inform her that she would give birth to a miracle baby. She replied, *"Yes sir if you say so, I believe!"*

The nurse asked me to leave so she could be transferred to another room. I left the hospital and headed home. Later that night, I received a call stating that Joann started feeling some discomfort in her stomach which prompted the staff to run more test. These test confirmed a fully developed fetus in her womb. She went on to carry the child nine months before delivering a healthy beautiful daughter. Today, her daughter, Tiffany Lewis is alive, healthy, and is the same age as my first child. In fact, they grew up together and she is now married with three healthy, beautiful children of her own.

One day, after devotion I was led to visit two relatives. An uncle who was an esteemed pastor. Another uncle who was a highly respected deacon. Both, highly respected for their scriptural knowledge. They each agreed I was teaching the truth, but warned me as a young man, to be careful going forward because religious leaders are territorial and dangerous. Especially, if they thought your message exposed them. Each of them committed to assist in guiding me and suggested I learn to work within church regulations to avoid conflict. Apparently, the damage among locals with whom I once had tremendous favor, was gone. I learned some of my messages offended secret societies, while others uncovered lifestyles that were totally oblivious to me.

I once thought preaching and teaching the truth would be the ultimate relationship bridge and soul-tie to a strong community presence. I was sadly mistaken. After I married Denise Odom in May 1981, we moved to our new home near Silver Bluff High School. I built an altar in the backyard surrounded by trees to visit daily for special time alone with God. As a prospect for pastor in one of the most prominent Baptist churches in the CSRA, I was asked to do a three-night revival. Although I declined the position, I did accept the engagement. Over 450 souls were converted that week during the revival and strong relationships were broken because I failed to consider their involvement in things exposed during the revival. Finally, I accepted Apostle Paul's rationale; *"If I please God, I will not please man."*

I learned the anointing of the Holy Spirit places anointed gifts in such a revelatory way that the vessel appears to know people's personal affairs and situations while ministering—*in spite of their ignorance.*

Paul said, *"For what man knows the things of a man, save the spirit of man which is in him? even so the things of God knows no man, but the Spirit of God,"* (1 Corinthians 2:11)

Here, a minister of the gospel may be totally oblivious to another's personal affairs and yet minister under the unction (or power of the Holy Spirit) as if they are very intimate and insightful of details without knowing those who are exposed or offended.

Lessons and Impartations:
Relationships with mentors and colleagues

I want to quote both, renown and unknown leaders who've impacted me in ways that shaped and influenced my leadership methods and strategies for years. Their wisdom and experiences served as the catalyst and constant revelation that I am now able to extract from whenever I'm in need. Although many are not mentioned in this particular project, I am grateful for their synergistic impartations which resurface whenever I'm without personal experience as a reference. My first teacher is Jesus Christ; my Savior and the Holy Spirit who is still today, my constant guide, my personal friend, and my most reliable consultant.

My first human Bible teacher, Uncle Sullivan Bush Sr., who pastor's five Baptist churches throughout the CSRA: *"Son, your heart to serve will never replace your need to know and understand the specific type of service God is calling you to do. How well you perform will be largely impacted by how well you know and operate within your personal assignment. I've seen many start passionately like you. They get in, get lost, get hurt, and get out!"*

Pastor CW Phinizy, my license and ordination shepherd and overseer of the Runs Missionary Baptist Church:

"Son make sure you know before you go. Many start in the ministry, but not all finish. Proof God's direction before you go and no devil on this side of hell will be able to stop you. And always watch your back, because the people you serve, can cause the greatest hurt you will ever experience. Trust only God, and be careful with all men."

One of My most consistent teachers over the span of my life and ministry has been, *Dr. Fredrick K. C. Price*, and a quote that has endured: *"When it comes to starting a ministry the first thing to do is find out what God wants you to do and let him direct you as to how you should start your ministry. There are many people pastoring who have no business pastoring because they never were waiting on God to direct them. God may be calling you to go work for someone else. In fact, your calling may be for you to assist another the rest of your life. That is a legitimate calling."*

"If I do not do something with my ministry or my life, then I am not going to succeed because God is not a failure. There is no way God can fail. There is too much failure in ministry, too many mediocre ministers. Some ministers remain mediocre throughout their lives, never really fulfilling what God has called them to do."

"If you succeed in ministry, it is not up to God, it is up to you. All of the ingredients for success are already here, and

He has given you a plan to follow so that you can succeed. When you succeed, God succeeds. When you fail, God fails, because people cannot see God. They can only see His so-called representatives. If the representatives of God are failures, then in the eyes of the world, God is a failure."

Apostle Darryl G. McCoy, founder and overseer of Trumpet in Zion Ministries International. Probably one of the most persistent and charismatic preachers of the gospel I've ever met. This man became the epitome of the saying, *"I will persist until I succeed."* He also consistently models the importance of fasting and prayer as necessary ingredients to a successful spiritual life and a consistent walk with God. A highly gifted and anointed preacher of faith. For several years, I watched him exercise precision in the prophetic and witnessed many miracle manifestations of healing from sickness, diseases, and deliverance from demonic spirits.

Apostle Marvin T. Boyd, probably my favorite preacher as a young man, along with Apostle Richard D. Henton. These two inspired me to become multi-faceted as a minister. They were notably studious, insightful, intense, fervent, skilled, and highly anointed men of God. Their every word seemingly sparked revelation in me. In other words, their messages always made me hungry for more of God!

Dr. Myles Munroe, shared with me on the set of WBPI, Watchmen Broadcast *"It is in this season of our time, that we, as stewards of this present age, must face the challenge of developing, training, releasing, and reproducing a generation of leaders who can secure the future for our children and their children. A good leader not only knows where he is going but can inspire others to go with him. Always remember, leadership is a privilege, influence is your resource."*

Dr. Tony Evans, quoted *"Leadership in the church is a given. You may have good or bad leaders, but having no leaders is not an option. For the church to function at all, someone has to lead, and someone else has to follow that's leadership."*

Dr. Creflo A. Dollar - Eagles Gathering 2002 stated *"The leader must realize the assignment is too big for his natural ability. If you do kingdom work without God, prepare to fail, because anything God authors He finishes."*

Bishop T. D. Jakes - stated, *"Overloaded people fail. They always have and they always will. They fail at marriage, ministry, and management. They fail at parenting, partnership, and professional endeavors. Like an airplane, we can only carry a certain amount of weight. If we have too much baggage on board, we will be ineffective and we won't be able to soar. Most people end up exceeding the weight limit. Motivated by the desire to please, impress, or otherwise gain commendation, they take on too much and, in the end, fail to reach the heights of success or else crash because they ignored their limitations."*

John C. Maxwell - Developing The Leader Around You, wrote: *"Great leaders; the truly successful ones who are in the top one percent, all have one thing in common. They know that acquiring and keeping good people is a leader's most important task. An organization cannot increase its productivity, but people can! The asset that truly appreciates within any organization is people. Systems become dated. Buildings deteriorate. Machinery wears. But people can grow, develop, and become more effective if they have a leader who understands their potential value."*

Terry Nance - God's Armor Bearer, Book II, Makes the point that, *"God wants his children to grow up and be like trees planted by the rivers of water. (Psalm 1:3) Have you ever noticed something peculiar about a tree? It never moves! We have beautiful pine trees on our church property, but I have never driven into the parking lot and found one of those trees moved overnight to a different place because it did not like where it was planted. Yet, in the body of Christ and even on church staff's, the first time someone is offended, he pulls up his roots and moves somewhere else, then wonders why there is no fruit in his life."*

My summary, as a teacher, preacher, motivator, life-coach, developer, mentor and trainer of many leaders for over three decades: I have personally discovered that, one of the most difficult things to tell an ignorant leader is something they *don't* know but *thinks* otherwise. It is also exceptionally hard to *train* a leader who *thinks* they don't need training.

For this reason, the words of Hosea the prophet should echo in our hearing frequently. So much so that it keeps us, as leaders, filled with a passion to pursue correct knowledge to establish right beliefs and lead or influence others effectively. Notice, "*My people are destroyed for lack of knowledge. Because you have rejected knowledge, I also will reject you from being priest for Me; Because you have forgotten the law of your God, I also will forget your children.*"

As stewards of the mysteries of God, we may take direction on how to divide the word of truth from our upbringing rather than the actual, scriptural "truth" in context. Which may provoke us in many cases to abstract kingdom leadership duty from privilege, instead of duty from principles and standards. The kingdom leader's duties are to only be drawn from their privileges, by way of inference, which corresponds solely with confirmable scriptural truths in context. The foundation of Christian practice must be laid in Christian knowledge and faith. This includes an understanding of the scope and operation of grace. But, we must first understand how we receive Christ Jesus the Lord, into our hearts and then we will know better how to walk in Him.

CHAPTER 3
AN AGELESS CONTRAST

The Gospel of Matthew 20:25-28 says, *"Jesus called His disciples to Himself and said, 'You know that the rulers of the Gentiles lord it over them, and those who are great exercise authority over them.*

Yet it shall not be so among you; but whoever desires to become great among you, let him be your servant. And whoever desires to be first among you, let him be your slave—just as the Son of Man did not come to be served, but to serve, and to give His life a ransom for many. '"

Can you be inconvenienced? Are you a leader who is not easily accessible or at hand when your organization or ministry duty demands immediate response? The Ministry of Christ and His Kingdom is about discipleship, serving, servicing, and developing His people. Many who desire to work for Him fail to realize the importance of servant-leadership which reflects His method and priorities. All who participate in kingdom leadership must look to Jesus as the ultimate model and example of servant leadership.

A kingdom leader's *mental* ability to retain conscious sight (memory) of the ways and methods of Jesus as their example, will become the leader's ability to implement or duplicate the kingdom way at all times. Especially, in challenging and testing times. Dr. Myles Munroe says, *"The principle of leadership is not self-serving but selfless service."* It is the opposite of selfish ambition; one which does not take others into consideration. *Servanthood* is the nature and attitude of true leaders.

To extrapolate Dr. Munroe's statement, notice how Jesus addressed kingdom leaders in Matthew 23:11,12, *"But he who is greatest among you shall be your servant. And whoever exalts himself will be humbled, and he who humbles himself will be exalted."* Here the word *servant-* (sur'-vant; 'ebhedh; doulos): is a very common word with a variety of meanings, all implying a greater or lesser degree of inferiority and desire of freedom.

The most frequent usage is the equivalent of *slave* (Genesis 9:25; 24:9; Exodus 21:5; Matthew 10:24; Luke 17:7). But also a hired workman or *"hired servant"* are Hebrew and Greek expressions which differ from the above. Its main focus is *"One who is distinguished as obedient and faithful to God or Christ."*

See Joshua 1:2; 2 Kings 8:19; Daniel 6:20; Colossians 4:12; 2 Timothy 2:24.

Servanthood and Leadership

In Matthew 25:31- 46, Jesus illustrated the importance of serving others as kingdom leaders. Clearly, the Testaments teaches that kingdom service requires: God first, others second and self, last. Notice Jesus says, *"When the Son of Man comes in His glory, and all the holy angels with Him, then He will sit on the throne of His glory. All the nations will be gathered before Him, and He will separate them one from another, as a shepherd divides his sheep from the goats. And He will set the sheep on His right hand, but the goats on the left. Then the King will say to those on His right hand, 'Come, you blessed of My Father, inherit the kingdom prepared for you from the foundation of the world: for I was hungry and you gave Me food; I was thirsty and you gave Me drink; I was a stranger and you took Me in; I was naked and you clothed Me; I was sick and you visited Me; I was in prison and you came to Me."*

"Then the righteous will answer Him, saying, 'Lord, when did we see You hungry and feed You, or thirsty and give You drink? When did we see You a stranger and take You in, or naked and clothe You? Or when did we see You sick, or in prison, and come to You?' And the KING will answer and say to them, 'assuredly, I say to you, inasmuch as you did it to one of the least of these my brethren, you did it to ME.'"

"Then He will also say to those on the left hand, 'Depart from Me, you cursed, into the everlasting fire prepared for the devil and his angels: for I was hungry and you gave Me

*no food; I was thirsty and you gave Me no drink; I was a
stranger and you did not take Me in, naked and you did not
clothe Me, sick and in prison and you did not visit Me.'*

*"Then they also will answer Him, saying, 'Lord, when
did we see You hungry or thirsty or a stranger or naked or
sick or in prison, and did not minister to You?' Then He will
answer them, saying, 'Assuredly, I say to you, inasmuch as
you did not do it to one of the least of these, you did not do it
to Me.' And these will go away into everlasting punishment,
but the righteous into eternal life."*

It is clear from these Scriptures; the judgment of the
great day will be a general judgment. People of all ages will
be summoned before Christ, from the beginning to the end
of time. The obvious distinction that will be made between
the righteous and the wicked servants is that *"He (Christ)
shall separate them one from another, as the tares and
wheat are separated at the harvest or the corn and chaff in
the floor."* Even though currently, wicked and godly dwell
together in the same kingdoms, cities, churches, families,
and are not easily distinguishable from one another; which
is also true regarding the infirmities of Saints and sinners,
the hypocrisies of sinners and Saints, and the difficulties of
maturity and progression of both.

But, in that day (the Day of the Lord) we will all be
separated, and parted forever; Malachi 3:18 says, *"Then shall
ye return, and discern between the righteous and the wicked."*
Even though, we cannot separate ourselves from one another

in this world (1 Corinthians 5:10), nor can anyone else separate us (1 Corinthians 13:29). The Lord knows them that are His and separates them. Jesus illustrated the importance of *serving* others. He emphasized servant-leadership directed by the will of God as necessary to be demonstrated and modeled to reflect our kingdom connection.

While it is clear that we are called to serve, not knowing the specificity of our call, the type of service or position we're called to, nor fully understanding the scope and perimeters of our assignments subjects many leaders to a perplexed life in ministry. It is all too obvious that church growth or ministry success has become a major hurdle for many ministers and leaders, marriages and families.

It is my belief that the foundational strength of all kingdom leaders' involvement begins with this thought; *To be effective in ministry requires a close and firm relationship with God for constant guidance and personal strength.*

Likewise, to be effective in marriage requires a close and firm relationship with God and your spouse for constant guidance and personal strength."

Without it you wear down and eventually wear out. Wisdom warns, *"You must keep your heart with all diligence."* These are certainly the two most important heart priorities. Ministers and leaders who maintain their ministry must be maintained by principles designed in Scripture and the people they serve. If not, the effective influence of that ministry will cease to be.

Alarming Statistics

Statistics from various reports indicate that pastors and their families are high-priority satanic targets today. While Holy Scripture warns, *"Whisperers and tale-bearers"* divide hierarchical relations. You, as leaders, must keep Scriptural order, discipline, and protocol to protect relational integrity. Especially, if you love and care for the bishops, pastors, and gifts God has ordained to watch over your souls.

Hebrews 13:7, 17, says *"Remember those who rule over you, who have spoken the word of God to you, whose faith follow, considering the outcome of their conduct Obey those who rule over you, and be submissive, for they watch out for your souls, as those who must give account. Let them do so with joy and not with grief, for that would be unprofitable for you."*

As we proceed throughout these pages you'll notice the frequent use of the words *order*, *discipline*, and *protocol* to convey Kingdom rule. Also, love, faith, and wisdom are mentioned to direct consistent kingdom character. However, before diving into the lesson, I'll share some interesting research. I was led to gather this information in support of my theory of the cause of kingdom leaders declining influence in today's society.

Research Supports Theory

I solicited this research from Berna, Focus on the Family, and Fuller Seminary. All of which backed up my findings and additional information from reviewing other's research to make the case that kingdom ministers and leaders are destroyed for lack of knowledge.

Reports also conclude that; Fifteen hundred pastors leave the ministry each month due to moral failure, spiritual burnout, or contention in their churches. Fifty percent of pastors' marriages end in divorce. Eighty percent of pastors feel unqualified and discouraged in their pastoral roles. Fifty percent of pastors are so discouraged, if they could, they would leave the ministry but have no other way of making a living. Eighty percent (80 percent) of seminary and Bible school graduates who enter the ministry, leave within the first five years. Seventy percent (70 percent) of pastor's battle depression and say the only time they study the Word is when preparing sermons (this is key).

Most statistics say that 60 to 80 percent of those entering the ministry leave ten years later. Only a fraction embraces it as a lifetime career. I believe over 90 percent of pastors start off as a true call with enthusiasm and the endurance of faith to make it. But something happens to derail their train of passion and love for the call. Focus on the Family reports that we, in the United States, lose a pastor a day as a result of him seeking an immoral path instead of God's; seeking intimacy where it must not be found.

F.O.F. statistics state that 70 percent of pastors don't have close personal friends, nor one in whom they can confide. The statistics I had with church growth resources are even higher. Pastors who tend to be very educated seem to embark on sin Saturdays and preach the Word on Sundays without conviction. It's also interesting that although 4000 new churches open each year, 7000 churches close each year. Clearly, the statistics indicate a tremendous need to revisit diverse Kingdom Principle Orientation and Training consistent with kingdom culture.

CHAPTER 4
BLURRED LINES: CHURCH
SUCCESS VS. FAMILY FAILURE

A great deal of chaos exists between pastoral leaders' personal, family, and professional lives. A leader's inability to prioritize their time often generates blurred lines. Failure to establish boundaries that protect and correspond with each entity results in a depreciation of one or each area eventually.

These blurred lines may be the reason a highly effective person experiences stress and ineffectiveness. Failure to bring balance and symmetry between the continual demands of family, occupation, and leadership may cause our inability to recognize many distracting devices that become destructive by invading our space and abusing our time.

In each case, before we solve the problem of a life without harmony we must first identify the problem, no matter how motivated we are to pursue our goals and demonstrate love and appreciation for our families and positions. Failure to structure our priorities and enforce boundaries against unwelcomed invaders and unnecessary activity will continue to cause leaders to spend more time and energy on things they care less about. My saying is, *"Life out of Order, is Life in Chaos!"* Because order is the one command that God has wisely given Kingdom leaders and Kingdom systems to be *governed by* and function *according to*. The concept of *"All things done decent and in order"* is to keep the leader's personal and positional life arranged in a way that preserves and protects both while maintaining an effective Kingdom system.

Ecclesiastes 10:10, says that *"If the ax is dull, and one does not sharpen the edge, then he must use more strength; But wisdom brings success."* The implication here is that wisdom teaches us to whet or sharpen the tool we intend to use, rather than leaving it blunt. A dull ax obliges us to exert more strength. We save ourselves excessive labor and avoid danger if we whet before we cut, or consider what are fit and appropriate principles to apply in every difficult case.

When we are trained in advance to pursue principle wisdom and commit to accountable references for assistance, it will guide us in properly sharpening our edge for those we lead, to avoid working deceitfully, while working cleanly and cleverly. Without careful cautious principle guidance and processing, leadership in ministry can become a very harsh and stressful responsibility.

During my first pastorate, I remember the multiple

challenges and unpredictable transitions that constantly had to be managed between ministry success and family stability. Sometimes it seemed as if it was impossible to experience success in both at the same time.

It's interesting that my illusion of easy success because of my most revered Scriptural knowledge, friendships with important people, gift to sing, preach, and draw large crowds became a setup for swift public success, but almost immediate private failure.

The church grew rapidly from tens to hundreds and the members and leaders were excited because of the significant growth we experienced. But, my most important ministry (marriage and family) was falling apart. Somehow I thought the fact that I sincerely loved and prized my wife and children above everything and everyone else was enough. I swiftly learned it wasn't. Although we sought mentors, we couldn't find any available locally at the time. We desperately needed guidance in prioritizing and balancing quality time between ministry and family. And our inability to establish priority communication and personal time together set the stage for many unanticipated adversities and challenges.

My wife Denise, felt neglected and overlooked, and I'll admit, she probably had good reason, but so did I. The children were young and in the middle of it all without a voice, waiting fearfully to see what the outcome would be. Our explosive conflicts grew from quarterly, to bi-monthly, to monthly. And finally, after a brief pause, we tried to pretend they were being silently managed and for the sake of the kids and leadership, nonexistent. Until they resurfaced and became weekly and daily challenges with major conflicts.

We eventually discovered that problems in relationships don't self-resolve and disappear just because we hope or wish they would. Like the addict or alcoholic who sometimes deceive themselves into thinking they can drown out their problems with substances. We thought pretending would help us escape. Only to realize those same problems were waiting and growing other bacteria and inconspicuous fungus. That would require more than simply, *"I love you,"* and *"I'm sorry."*

Apologies started to feel like set-ups, not to be relied upon, or to put much stock in. Life at home was growing cold and isolated in spite of the noise and interaction with the children. Everything became a point of contention regardless of how good or bad it was on the surface. We disagreed so much that we learned how to disagree about our disagreements. One day, after going to the bookstore to pick up a divorce application because of a heated argument that almost became a war zone. I told her I was going to prepare the papers and before I knew it she went and got her a female attorney.

Thank God we survived by His abundant Grace.

Putting off the Inevitable
Cost vs. Value

I included this section because it was necessary to speak to the senior leader's inability, refusal, or avoidance in removing ineffective leaders who become an obvious cost to the team in many ways. It is mainly a friendly reminder that Putting off the inevitable usually results in the person who should be removed or replaced becoming the person who sabotages the relational chemistry of an otherwise effective team. Simply because their destructive behavior is tolerated much longer than is required.

Remember, leaven spreads and becomes infectious to other team members. Which ultimately, may result in a non-existent ministry. In the same chapter that Adam and Eve transgressed against their position with God, they were judged, sentenced, and removed to demonstrate the importance of protecting the Garden at all cost. Genesis 3:23-24 says, *"Therefore the LORD God sent him out of the garden of Eden to till the ground from which he was taken. So He drove out the man; and He placed cherubim at the east of the garden of Eden, and a flaming sword which turned every way, to guard the way to the tree of life."*

A few years ago, I had to remove a person I liked very much, from a very strategic position, because of their ineffectiveness. After consulting and deliberating with the team of directors and deacons, I actually thought I employed the wisest most caring way to maneuver this position without provoking adversity around the person or position.

Even though I anticipated some decline in the leader's interest and operation towards the ministry, I'd never considered the possibility of this person using their position to influence a sentiment against other leaders that would result in large segments of the ministry silently, questioning my authority and methods. Sometimes we think that our obvious personal investments of time, monetary, material and spiritual things beyond the call of duty will prevent such folly. But, I was in for a rude awakening.

As strange as it seemed, initially, the leader's removal was prompted by constant conflict with other senior leaders and staff directors who constantly manifested their suspicions as they grew tired of working with them. Their frustration led to speculation and accusations begin to surface against the leader in staff meetings which pointed towards the reason several quality leaders had suddenly left the ministry.

Early Warning Signs

My point is that the Holy Spirit along with family members, a few pastors and covenant partners had all been trying to get my attention for several months before I decided to remove the leader. Looking for ways to deflect and direct a negative light away from the leader's family was very important to me because I wanted them to be comfortable, inclusive members. But against the advice of senior directors and leaders, I became so consumed with that one family's membership comfort, that I vacated the principle of securing the interest of the ministry first and I neglected the principle of cost over value.

So, while I looked out for the leader and their family, the offended leader looked for ways to dismantle the ministry I'd worked so hard to build with my life and sacrifices. With lies, deceptions, whispers, etc. Each time I confronted the leader, they couldn't seem to understand why or where the rumors came from. My disappointment was at an *all-time high*! Because I'd never considered that this person I'd developed a relaxed confidence in, could *lie* so casually. One day, I gathered my facts and confronted the person face-to-face for the second time.

To be truthful, I felt stupid, because I'd been warned. I knew better, and I neglected to adhere to insightful staff members. Those whose proven love, loyalty and commitment to the ministry for years were very disturbed by experiences they had and situations they were intimately aware of from other leaders.

There's a saying among leaders training at Quantico, a division of the FBI; quote *"You can sell anything you want to if you have enough help."* That is exactly what the demoted leader did. Eventually, this person doubled-back, and established undercover relationships with the leader's they formerly resented, complained about frequently, and stayed in constant conflict with, to generate hidden allies within the staff.

At the time, the ministry experienced tremendous momentum and growth. Our numbers peaked between 700 and 750. When the decline started I was so distracted by other ministry projects that I failed to notice members were leaving or simply losing interest in attending this *dynamic ministry* I was sure they were all proud to be a part of.

So much nonsense and chaos manifested among the ministry's senior staff leaders. I was led by the Holy

Spirit to dismantle the Executive Board and relieve them of their duties. Suddenly, unaccountable communication breakdowns, revelations of inappropriate behavior of deacon and member relationships, abuses of power, whispers against hierarchal positions, unscriptural practices, and cover-ups surfaced that demanded correction and immediate changes.

Throughout an entire season, things continued to manifest that drastically changed the dynamics and peaceful construct of what once was considered as highly effective leadership relations. Even though God abundantly blessed and sustained the ministry during this period. The chaos did not cease until all of the adversely-affected senior staff left the ministry. Which included the former assistant pastor, deacon chair, youth pastor, intercessory lead, and technology department leader. With the exception of the youth pastor and technology leader who became casualties of war, it was inevitable that all the other positions be silenced.

Today my failure to execute swiftly what was inevitably the necessary removal of three primary ministry positions became a priceless lesson to both me and the ministry I serve. Looking back, these three position-holders always had problems with the ministry's protocol and accountability systems. I pray seniors will not take for granted what must inevitably happen. Execute before your *cost* far outweighs the *value* of the leader who needs to be removed expeditiously. Putting off the inevitable one who should be removed, results in that one sabotaging an otherwise effective team.

Beware of Burnout

Another word of caution; if constant stresses of ministry have you feeling disillusioned, helpless, and completely worn out, it may be from burnout. When you're burned out, problems seem insurmountable, everything looks bleak, and it's difficult to muster up the energy to care—*let alone do something about your situation.* The *unhappiness* and *detachment* burnout can threaten marriages, ministries, relationships, and health.

But burnout can be healed. You can regain your balance by reassessing priorities, making time for yourself, and seeking support. What is burnout? It's a state of emotional, mental, and physical exhaustion caused by excessive and prolonged stress. It occurs when feeling overwhelmed and unable to meet the demands of family and ministry consistently. As stress continues, it is easy to lose interest and motivation for the office you took on in the first place.

Psychologist say that burnout reduces productivity, zaps energy, and leaves you feeling helpless, hopeless, cynical, and resentful. Eventually, you might feel you have nothing more to give.

Most of us have challenging days. Those days when dragging ourselves out of bed seems to require the strength of Hercules. If you feel like this most of the time, you might have burnout. Particularly if, every day is a bad day; caring about work and home seems like a waste of energy. You're exhausted all the time. The majority of your day is spent on tasks you find either mind-numbing or overwhelming. You feel like the things you do makes no difference or is under-appreciated.

The negative effects of burnout spill over into every area of life—including home and social life. Burnout can also negatively impact the body leaving you vulnerable to illnesses. Because of its many consequences, it's important to deal with burnout right away.

Dealing with Burnout
The three -*R's*- approach
1. *Recognize* – watch for the warning signs of burnout
2. *Reverse* – undo the damage by managing stress and seeking support
3. *Resilience* – build resilience to stress. Take care of your physical and emotional health.

The difference between stress and burnout is, burnout may be the result of unrelenting stress, but it isn't the same as too much stress. Stress, by and large, involves too much: too many pressures demanding more of you physically and psychologically than you have. Stressed people might deceive themselves thinking if they get everything under control, they'll feel better. Burnout, on the other hand, is about not having enough. Burnout means feeling empty, devoid of motivation, and beyond caring.

People experiencing burnout often don't see any hope of positive change in their situations. If excessive stress is like drowning in responsibilities, burnout is being all dried up.

While you're aware of being under stress, you don't always notice burnout when it happens. The constant and shifting challenges of leadership gradually become wearisome and overwhelming anytime you take too much upon yourself. Be conscious of your continual need to live with balance and refuse to co-exist without a support system.

Prepare for Success

Someone once said, *"To be successful, you must do what the successful do."* So before I could gather these objects I was led to study and closely examine the lives of kingdom leaders who witness both great success and failure. A selection which includes patriarchs and matriarchs *Abraham, Isaac, Jacob, Joseph, Naomi* and *Esther* whose personal lives demanded character changes in order to succeed in leading their families and personal servants.

Next, I chose *Moses, Joshua, Gideon, Jephthah, Eli, Samuel, David, Solomon, Elijah, Elisha, Jesus, Peter,* and *Paul* as corporate models. Then from these leaders, I extracted these qualities and attributes that made them most effective in their seasons of success. It's also apparent that each time they strayed from these objects, they declined in their assignments and became ineffective leaders.

I concluded that to prevent failure, success must consume your focus and efforts. Because failure is a temporary encounter. We may all enhance our ability to succeed by redefining with precision, our true target in our assignments.

CHAPTER 5
COVENANT PARTNERSHIP

"Those who cannot conceive or grasp the operation of grace in the kingdom, will not properly walk by faith."

Jesus describes the Kingdom of God as a social order in which the relationship of men to God, is like that of sons to a father and their relation to each other like that between brothers.

This social ideal, which presents itself vividly and continuously to His mind, is summed up in this phrase, "Kingdom of God," which occurs more than a hundred times in the Synoptic Gospels. The passages form the interior climax of His message to men. It is a kingdom of God *within you,* and the chief element of it is communion with God.

Leadership operation in the Kingdom of God is for tough-minded people because you will be challenged by every oppositional principle.

Matthew 6:33, is a call to covenant partnership with the supernatural for the purpose of totally transforming your entire life as a leader to reflect Heaven on Earth. Here, I've listed six principles to remember.

1. Everything Jesus faced He looked to heaven first for an answer. He demonstrated how to live in contact with an entirely different world and realm beyond the natural.

2. Heaven must become your primary resource: Deuteronomy 8:18, and Ephesians 1:3 says, *you are not limited to earth's resources.*

3. To *first seek* is to depend on your partnership with God to answer *all* of Earth's Crisis. Philippians 4:19 *"And my God shall supply all your needs according to His riches in glory by Christ Jesus."*

4. Everything we need is stored in a realm which cannot be seen, it requires faith. Hebrews 11:1-3; Habakkuk 2:2-4; Romans 1:16, 17; Hebrews 10 and 2 Corinthians 5:7.

5. God's way: God has seed for everything you need. This means we plant heaven in the earth by setting Heaven above Earth. In this, we honor God's authority in us as co-creator through us. Speak the word!

6. Angels wait to do God's bidding for us on the Earth. Proverbs 16:7; Psalms 103:20 *"Bless the LORD, you His angels, who excel in strength, who do His word, heeding the voice of His word."*

The Importance of Partnership

The Scriptures prove that God has never done anything in the earth realm without the partnership of man. This is a primary reason He lives within us. For me, Mark 6:5-6 is one of the most shocking Scriptures in the Bible. Notice, *"And Jesus could do no work of power there, except that He laid His hands on a few sick ones, He healed them. And He marveled because of their unbelief. And He went around the villages, in a circuit, teaching."*

From this, we extract a principle truth. "God has limited His unlimited ability to our *faith*." A principle which implies there are some things God cannot do. Even though, many of us may have a hard time agreeing with this truth. It is an absolute truth which the Holy Scripture in context, plainly supports. Example, according to Isaiah 55, God can't think like we think, He is omniscient which means He already knows everything all the time. He never has to think in order to figure out what to do next or what direction to take as we do.

Another thing, God's healing can't work without faith. Notice, James 5:14, 15 says, *"Is anyone among you sick? Let him call for the elders of the church, and let them pray over him, anointing him with oil in the name of the Lord. And the prayer of faith will save the sick, And the Lord will raise him up. And if he has committed sins, he will be forgiven."*

Lastly, it is also clear that God cannot fulfill the mandate of the commission without our partnership with Him. Notice, *"And Jesus came and spoke to them, saying,* "All authority has been given to Me in heaven and on earth. *Go therefore and make disciples of all the nations, baptizing them in the name of the Father and of the Son, and of the Holy Spirit, teaching them to observe all things that I have commanded you; and lo, I am with you always, even to the end of the age. Amen.*" (Matthew 28:18-20, *NKJV*)

In this, Jesus invites His twelve apostles to go as partners in His stead and make disciples of all the nations. Then He promises to be with them to the end of the age. With this in mind, as Kingdom Leaders there are three things to remember:

1. God will never do our part.
2. Our part is never supernatural (our part is the natural, God's part is the supernatural).
3. Our part is first because God has already done His part. For instance, Jesus will never die again. So it's time to do your part.

Although, many times through ignorance we get upset with God because He won't do our part. The fact is, His involvement with us is about partnership. Look at Luke 5:1-11. I call this a lesson for the ages.

Points to Ponder

It helps to remember what God instructs us to do and what we cannot do without Him. His instructions locate and identify His grace in our lives and situations. This was my experience while stopping by the waiting room at the hospital with Joann Lewis. Her husband had called me back that same night overjoyed and shouting, *"Man you won't believe what the doctors just confirmed! She is still pregnant! This woman is still pregnant and we're having our first baby! Are you coming back?"* He inquired. *"No, not right now, it's God's miraculous power that needs to be celebrated."*

Now from this, we see that those who cannot conceive the operation of grace in the Kingdom will not properly walk by faith. This is why ministry leaders must be established in right perspective.

Three Covenant Essentials

From Genesis to Revelation the Bible establishes three essentials for our conceptual understanding. The King, Kingdom, and the King's royal offspring, which includes us. This is why Matthew 18:23, says, *"Therefore the kingdom of heaven is like a certain king who wanted to settle accounts with his servants."* As the king's servants, we are considered His sons who are stewards over His accounts. Revelation 17:14, says, *"for He is Lord of lords and King of kings; and those who are with Him are Called, Chosen, and Faithful."*

Notice the three characteristics of stewards/sons:

1. Called. 2. Chosen. 3. Faithful.

We must constantly challenge ourselves as kingdom leaders to live by faith, as the currency of the kingdom and to be honest and faithful stewards over everything and everyone. When you understand the three characteristics of kingdom steward-sons, then you realize there is absolutely no reason, as partners with God, to doubt, worry, fear, seek revenge, practice unforgiveness, hold back, or rob God.

In John 17:16, Jesus established that we are not of this world, as He is not. Since we then are not of this world, it is important to learn what governs ours to enjoy its benefits and privileges. In Matthew 16:19, Jesus said, *"And I will give you the keys of the kingdom of Heaven, and whatever you bind on Earth will be bound in Heaven, and whatever you loose on Earth will be loosed in Heaven."*

These keys are faith, laws, principles, precepts, ordinances, sayings, and systems that illustrate how the kingdom functions through God's grace. But, here again, you must learn and apply them as citizens in order to gain their benefits and privileges. In Matthew 16, Jesus says *"I give you keys,"* meaning the kingdom is accessible but to access it you must have specific keys to get in. You can stand at the door knowing the benefits are just on the other side, but be unable to enter because you don't have the keys. Keys are the access to a higher level of availability to our Lord Jesus Christ. In dealing with the kingdom there are a number of things we must first grasp; the kingdom manifests itself in various levels. If life is lived on levels and is experienced in stages, it is also established in dimensions.

This is the primary reason Jesus said in Matthew 6:33 and 34, *"But seek first the kingdom of God and his righteousness, and all these things shall be added to you. Therefore, do not worry about tomorrow, for tomorrow will worry about its own things. Sufficient for the day is its own trouble."*

Notice how the Message Bible explains it: *"Steep your life in God-reality, God-initiative, God-provisions. Don't worry about missing out. You'll find all your everyday human concerns will be met. Give your entire attention to what God is doing right now, and don't get worked up about what may or may not happen tomorrow. God will help you deal with whatever hard things come up when the time comes."*

When we talk about the Kingdom of God and the issues of dominion God gave us in Genesis 1:26-28, we must understand and remember; dominion is a process. Not a magic wand. Just as seeking the Kingdom of God and His righteousness is a lifetime pursuit for a lifestyle conformance. It literally takes *time* to achieve areas of *dominion* because it is a process.

In the dominion process, God requires kingdom citizens representing Him as Christians in the world's social system or cosmos, to be disciplined. Realize, you cannot be an effective Christian undisciplined because the commission is about *making disciplines*. That's why the Bible says in Matthew 28:18-19, *"And Jesus came and spoke to them, saying, "All authority has been given to Me in heaven and on earth. Go therefore and make disciples of all the nations."* The mere fact that we have to make disciples implies the need to live a disciplined life. Which is in kingdom citizenship, a regimented walk.

To make this clear, in the kingdom of God, as we aspire to serve the Lord Jesus Christ it is here that we deny all of our rights, and place our focus on becoming submissive to a new order within the scope of God's Kingdom. The deal is that new life in the Christian's world is supposed to be life submitted to this new order. That *new order* is kingdom dominion mentioned in the Old Testament, which is the offspring of the righteousness of God in the New Testament.

A lack of order, discipline, and protocol is the primary reason today's Believers may exist without manifestation to confirm their *faith* or conform to a highly productive Kingdom lifestyle. Without discipline, we cannot properly attain authority. My daily hope is for kingdom order to be restored in the Body of Christ, especially in places where *true Believers* worship, because we cannot influence the world system without kingdom discipline.

Romans 12:1, 2 says, "*I appeal to you therefore, brethren, and beg of you in view of [all] the mercies of God, to make a decisive dedication of your bodies [presenting all your members and faculties] as a living sacrifice, holy (devoted, consecrated) and well pleasing to God, which is your reasonable (rational, intelligent) service and spiritual worship.*

Do not be conformed to this world (this age), [fashioned after and adapted to its external, superficial customs], but be transformed (changed) by the [entire] renewal of your mind [by its new ideals and its new attitude], so that you may prove [for yourselves] what is the good and acceptable and perfect will of God, even the thing which is good and acceptable and perfect [in His sight for you]."

A System of Commonwealth

In covenant partnership, understand that the Kingdom of God is a system of commonwealth because it is the King's commitment to ensure that *all* His citizens have access to the wealth and resources of the Kingdom. In this, the quality of *life* of the King's citizens reflect both His *glory* and *reputation*. Psalm 84:11 says, *"For the Lord God is a sun and shield; The Lord will give grace and glory; no good thing will He withhold from those who walk uprightly."* Matthew 6:30-32 (*Message*), says *"If God gives such attention to the appearance of wildflowers-most of which are never even seen don't you think He'll attend to you, take pride in you, do his best for you?"*

Don't be preoccupied with *getting*, to *respond* to God's *giving*. People who don't know God and the way He works tend to fuss over these things, but you know both God and how He works. Form your purpose by asking for counsel, then carry it out using all the help you can get." (Proverbs 20:18, *Message*)

The Kingdom's Economy

In the last part of this chapter, I want to encourage *leaders* to stay grounded in your faithfulness to the kingdom's economy and taxation systems because in God's grace system your *response* and *participation* determines the *manifestation* of your benefits and prosperity. Note, all kingdoms incorporate a taxation system, which allows its citizens to maintain its infrastructure. It is faithfulness to this system which allows the citizenship of a kingdom, access to investment opportunities, and creative development programs designed to prosper and share a *kingdom's commonwealth.*

This is why Jesus said in Luke 6:38, *"Give, and it will be given to you: good measure, pressed down, shaken together, and running over will be put into your bosom. For with the same measure that you use, it will be measured back to you."* In Matthew 22:17, 20-22 the Pharisees said, *"Tell us then, what is your opinion? Is it right to pay the imperial tax to Caesar or not?"* and he asked them, *"Whose image is this? And whose inscription?"* *"Caesar's,"* they replied. Then he said to them, *"So give back to Caesar what is Caesar's, and to God what is God's."*

When they heard this, they were amazed. So they left him and went away.

Notice Malachi 3:8-12, *"Will a mere mortal rob God? Yet you rob me. But you ask, 'How are we robbing you?' In tithes and offerings. You are under a curse—your whole nation—because you are robbing me. Bring the whole tithe into the storehouse, that there may be food in my house. Test me in this, says the Lord Almighty, and see if I will not throw open the floodgates of heaven and pour out so much blessing that there will not be room enough to store it."*

God will prevent pests from devouring your crops, and the vines in your fields will not drop their fruit before it is ripe. He further says, then all the nations will call you blessed, for yours will be a delightful land. (Malachi 3:8-12, *NIV*) In Matthew 23:23 Jesus called the Pharisees hypocrites, stating, *"For you pay tithe of mint and anise and cumin, and have neglected the weightier matters of the law: justice and mercy and faith."*

These *you ought not to have done*, without leaving the others undone. In conclusion for now, as a kingdom *leader*, understand that all these work together to bring the principles of provision and royal favor. In all kingdoms, the kings are *obligated* to provide security and welfare for His citizens at His own expense. This principle of handling treasure is actually the same principle God has elected to establish; heart, trust, and relational honor.

If you can grasp this, you will understand why David said, *"I have been young, and now I am old; Yet I have not seen the righteous forsaken, nor his descendants begging bread."* He is ever merciful and lends, and his descendants are blessed. (Psalm 37:25, 26) In this, we establish that God's divine partnership prerogative as the sovereign King is that He may extend a personal law to a citizen to receive special privileges and advantages protected solely by Him, at any and all times by *grace*.

His sons were included with him in the duty of caring for sacrificial rites and things. They served in receiving and presenting the various offerings and could enter and serve in the first chamber of the Tabernacle. But only Aaron, the high priest, called the Mediator of the Old Covenant, could enter into the Holy of Holies only once a year, on the great Day of Atonement. (Leviticus 16:12-14)

CHAPTER 6
THE OBJECTS OF KINGDOM LEADERSHIP

*"God is Spirit, and those who worship Him
must worship in spirit and truth."*

A few years ago in a leadership luncheon, as senior pastors and leaders sought ways to train and develop their leadership teams using kingdom principles, I was asked questions about the foundation of Kingdom leadership. The question was, in order to fulfill our commission of producing kingdom disciples and keeping them, what are the primary or foundational objects that should govern and regulate true and authentic kingdom leadership?

How do objects distinguish kingdom leaders from worldly leaders? How can these objects influence the survival of clergy and family unity to relieve the frustrating passions of the most central ministers and leaders in each kingdom assignment? One of the younger pastorate teams seemed to barely hold on. The couple had only been in the senior position three years and were already contemplating divorce and retirement from ministry.

Another seasoned pastor survived a church split that left his family severely fractured and burned-out. To be honest, a few years earlier I had difficulty believing my own family would survive the many dysfunctions of ministry, family, and leadership. After several days of prayer and fasting, Bible study and meditation, I had intense discussions and deliberation with senior and associate pastors, ministers, and a broad variety of ordained clergy.

During this time, the answer became clear to me. These were essential to direct the approach and posture of ministry leaders in order to preserve the relational unity of pastors' families and to interrupt the dissolution of congregations throughout the world. So, I began this project by clarifying and defining what an *object* was and how it is used to influence attitudes, systems, processes, behaviors, and other characteristics that determine kingdom entities and organizational success.

By definition, an *object* is anything that is visible or tangible and is relatively stable in form. It is a thing, person, or matter to which thought or action is directed. An object from this perspective is also the end; which *effort* or *action* is directed; it is the goal and purpose of which a thing exists. In light of this we can say, as profit is a primary object of business, so establishing and advancing the Kingdom of God and its citizenship must become the primary object of preaching and teaching of the Gospel, and the sole purpose of all ministry missions, systems, methods, or applications, and church fellowship.

As I introduce the objects keep in mind that these are not the only objects to kingdom or successful leadership. But, each of these are significantly important and should definitely be integrated into the character, practices, and postures of all leaders.

Objects of Leadership

These objects are listed with consideration of each kingdom leader having an already established personal relationship with God through Christ Jesus our Lord and Savior.

- Object 1: Consistent prayer life. A Kingdom leader must be constant in prayer, study, meditation, and obedience to develop a spiritual life. (Romans 8:14)

- Object 2: Right perspective. A spiritual leader must lead by *vision* that clarifies and makes tangible the missions and plans of the ministry. Although the Holy Spirit is our guide, the majority of the church is carnal and requires vision to make leadership tangible and comprehensible for involvement. (Proverbs 29:18; Habakkuk 2:2-4)

- Object 3: Right activity. Kingdom *vision* demands *faith*. While objects two and three are interchangeable because one without the other loses strength and focus eventually for lack of concept.

I wrestle with the order because although we walk by faith, without vision, faith is blind. Kingdom vision demands faith, and faith is immaterial without vision. This is why some leaders lack the ability to transfer their intentions to team members in a way they can conceive and conform to effectively assist them.

- Object 4: Love and right motive. Kingdom faith works by love. In spiritual matters, faith needs vision or its blind-faith. Faith must also be motivated by love to make it profitable for all Kingdom service and to make the servant a representative of God.

- Object 5: Wisdom and right direction. Kingdom *love* demands *wisdom*. The principle thing that gives all qualities, values, standards, methods, systems, and operations logical significance for cohesion and coordination to work together in right timing for accomplishment and effective involvement.

- Object 6: Right oversight. The principle of spiritual covering. Authority, honor, and submission are interlocking principles designed to assist leaders in becoming disciplined and loyal to the spiritual demands of Kingdom authority, order, and protocol. (1 Corinthians 14:40)

- Object 7: Right foundation and principle of grace. You are graced for it. Understanding the divine existence and operation of grace, both defines and simplifies the purpose for the leader and the specific service they are called to.

- Object 8: Right spirit. Principle of self-denial.
- Object 9: Maturity test. The big 'O' of offense.
- Object 10: The principle of *steadfastness.*
- Object 11: The principle of self-temperance. The Word must regulate kingdom leader's desires and motives to constantly glorify God.
- Object 12: Leadership habits. The twelve *be-habits.* 1 Peter 5:8-10 warns kingdom citizens to *"Be sensible and vigilant, because your adversary the Devil walks about like a roaring lion, seeking someone he may devour; who firmly resist in the faith, knowing that the same afflictions in the world are being completed in your brotherhood. But the God of all grace, He's calling us to His eternal glory by Christ Jesus, after you have suffered a little, He will perfect, confirm, strengthen, and establish you."*

Peter also admonishes, *"Simon Peter, a bondservant and apostle of Jesus Christ, to those who have obtained like precious faith with us by the righteousness of our God and Savior Jesus Christ: Grace and peace be multiplied to you in the knowledge of God and of Jesus our Lord, as His divine power has given to us all things that pertain to life and godliness, through the knowledge of Him who called us by glory and virtue, by which have been given to us exceedingly great and precious promises, that through these you may be partakers of the divine nature, having escaped the corruption that is in the world through lust. But also for this very reason, giving all diligence, add to your faith virtue, to virtue knowledge, to knowledge self-control, to self-control perseverance, to perseverance godliness, to godliness brotherly kindness, and to brotherly kindness love. For if these things are yours and abound, you will be neither barren nor unfruitful in the knowledge of our Lord Jesus Christ. For he who lacks these things is shortsighted, even to blindness, and has forgotten that he was cleansed from his old sins. Therefore, brethren, be even more diligent to make your call and election sure, for if you do these things you will never stumble; for so an entrance will be supplied to you abundantly into the everlasting kingdom of our Lord and Savior Jesus Christ."* (2 Peter 1:1-11, *NKJV*)

The Importance of Objects

Often what happens in the Body of Christ is that many fail through the church, because untested traditions are often practiced. To grasp the concept of *Kingdom* and the primary place it must hold in our lives and daily affairs think of what Jesus said to the Samaritan woman in John 4:21-24, *"Woman, believe Me, the hour is coming when you will neither on this mountain, nor in Jerusalem, worship the Father. You worship what you do not know; we know what we worship, for salvation is of the Jews. But the hour is coming, and now is, when the true worshipers will worship the Father in spirit and truth; for the Father is seeking such to worship Him. God is Spirit, and those who worship Him must worship in spirit and truth."*

86

Here He alluded to the fact that *true worship* has a distinct purpose which establishes a bridge that connects Kingdom fatherhood with its born-again sons. Another focus in the discussion regarding the essence of true worship is the establishment of sons over disciples. Notice how *The Message* emphasizes verse 22: "*You worship guessing in the dark; we Jews worship in the clear light of day.*"

Again notice how the *Amplified* clarifies the stifling impact of *not knowing.* "*You [Samaritans] do not know what you are worshiping [you worship what you do not comprehend]. We do know what we are worshiping [we worship what we have knowledge of and understand].*" From these passages, the statement of Hosea the prophet echoes throughout the church world ecumenically: "*My people are destroyed for lack of knowledge.*"

Pay close attention to what willful ignorance promotes. Hosea further states, "*Because you [the priestly nation] have rejected knowledge, I will also reject you that you shall be no priest to me; seeing you have forgotten the law of your God, I will also forget your children.*" (*AMP*) In Peter's second letter to the church, he established that understanding the grace and peace factors are essential for all Kingdom citizens and leaders. They are each multiplied through knowledge.

Second Peter 1:3: "*For His divine power (Grace) has bestowed upon us all things that [are requisite and suited] to life and godliness, through the [full, personal] knowledge of Him who called us by and to His own glory and excellence (virtue)."* Understanding the concept of Kingdom matters include the operation of grace accompanied by the confirmation of peace, must begin to impact us individually, collectively as families, and corporately as ministry teams and church communities. *"There is nothing as powerful as a concept, and nothing more dangerous than a misconception."* (Author unknown)

In this case, those who cannot conceive Kingdom matters, will not walk according to the objects that govern them. It must be clear that when we mistake the Word of God or misunderstand these principles, we risk our operations [individually and corporately] by living in religious self-deceit by our own futile efforts and allow the god of this world the opportunity to reign as chief influence in our lives as leaders and ultimately to *"Blind the minds of all who fail or refuse to believe."*

But, for those who understand the concept of Kingdom matter, it first becomes clear that as children of God, we are in this world but not of *it*. The fact is, there are natural kingdoms and spiritual kingdoms that co-exist in this reality. As Jesus answered Pilate, by saying, *"My kingdom (kingship, royal power) belongs not to this world. If my kingdom were of this world, my followers would have been fighting to keep Me from being handed over to the Jews. But as it is, my kingdom is not from here (this world); [it has no such origin or source]."* (John 18:36, *AMP*)

From this, we see that the natural kingdom functions and

takes its reality, by natural, visible things, that require the use of the natural senses to confirm their existence. Such as things you touch, taste, smell, etc. While the spiritual kingdom functions and takes its reality by grace using spiritual invisible words, described as life and truth words of faith, which are actually things. But these Spirit-filled words are things that are exposed and revealed by the logos or written Word of God and the Holy Spirit which leads and guides the Believer into all truth.

These words through scriptural knowledge, convey both what the unseen reality houses or consist of, and how it operates. Apostle Paul confirms this point; *"But as it is written: Eye has not seen, nor ear heard, nor have entered into the heart of man the things which God has prepared for those who love Him."* But God has revealed them to us through His Spirit. For the Spirit searches all things, yes, the deep things of God. For what man knows the things of a man except for the spirit of the man which is in him? Even so, no one knows the things of God except the Spirit of God.

Now we have received, not the spirit of the world, but the Spirit who is from God, that we might *know the things* that have been freely given to us by God." (1 Corinthians 2:9-12)

The reason the born-again (the just) live and walk by faith is because faith activates grace which bridges our understanding by becoming the actual substance of our new reality and by giving us knowledge, belief, trust, and the tangible ability, to stay in touch with what is real in our kingdom at all times.

This is why Jesus said, *my kingdom is not of this world. In the world you shall have tribulation, in Me you might have Peace.* In other words, in the natural realm or world, as long as we (children of God) are here, we must realize that all nature knows that Kingdom citizens now live in a more superior system through the grace of the redemptive work of Christ. But, this satanically influenced system will constantly trouble and test us to interfere with our rest and peace, to make us disbelieve we are what God says about us through grace.

This is why all kingdom citizens and especially leaders, must progress in Word- or faith-knowledge and pray for wisdom and revelation to always be aware of who we are, who's we are, what we have, and what we can do, as the *just*, who live by *faith*! Countless times *leadership* is identified as being out of touch with *who* and *what* it is responsible for representing in its service and involvement in ministry and church affairs.

This is why Hebrews 11:6 (*MSG*) says, *"It's Impossible to please God apart from faith."* Why? Because anyone who wants to approach God must believe both that He exists and that He cares enough to respond to those who diligently seek Him. Since pleasing God is our primary focus, faith is most essential because it's the substance that *underwrites* all involvement and activity with God and the supernatural realm.

Notice how Jesus addressed the disciples being trained and mentored in Mark 4:35-40: *"On the same day, when evening had come, He said to them, 'Let us cross over to the other side.' Now when they had left the multitude, they took Him along in the boat as He was. And other little boats were also with Him. And a great windstorm arose, and the waves beat into the boat, so that it was already filling. But He was in the stern, asleep on a pillow. And they awoke Him and said to Him, 'Teacher, do you not care that we are perishing?' Then He arose and rebuked the wind, and said to the sea, 'Peace, be still!' And the wind ceased and there was a great calm. But He said to them, 'Why are you so fearful? How is it that you have no faith?'"*

If, as ministry leaders, we don't model and demonstrate our dependence on grace through *faith* to those we serve, what *imitations* do we encourage to those who follow us? Notice, Jesus was in the stern, asleep on a pillow. But, the disciples kept their eyes on the storm instead of their leader who became a model for them in the midst of the turbulence. It is safe to say, that if we watch or continue to keep our focus on the turbulence of the storms which arise in ministry, this determines our failures. But if we keep our eyes on Christ; the God of all grace, the principles of the kingdom will determine our success.

CHAPTER 7
OBJECTS IN DETAIL

People today want privileges without problems,
Blessings without Sacrifice, which may result in a Life
with a God-form that denies the true God's Power.

The Kingdom of God is God's invisible spirit realm and rule in the Earth. Since the Kingdom is a Spirit-filled invisible realm, the objects that govern it must embody the context of the Spirit to successfully guide and account for it. Jesus said to the Jewish leader, Nicodemus, "*I tell you the truth, unless you are born again, you cannot see the Kingdom of God. 'What do you mean?'*" exclaimed Nicodemus. "*How can an old man go back into his mother's womb and be born again?*"

Jesus replied, "*I assure you, no one can enter the Kingdom of God without being born of water and the Spirit.*" Humans can reproduce human life, but the Holy Spirit gives birth to *Spiritual* life. So, don't be surprised when I say, 'You must be *born again.'* (John 3:3-7, *NLT*)

An *object* is an *end* which *effort* or *action* is directed; it is the goal and purpose for which a thing exists. As profit is the object of business, so advancing the Kingdom of God must become the primary *object* of preaching the Gospel and the sole purpose for ministry methods or applications and Church fellowship.

Objects of Kingdom Leadership Explored

It is my belief that the foundational underpinning of all kingdom leader's involvement begins with this thought: *"To be effective in ministry requires a close and firm relationship with God, for constant guidance and personal strength."* Without it, you wear down and wear out. Wisdom warns, *"You must keep your heart with all diligence."* The ministers and leaders who maintain the ministry must be maintained or that ministry will cease to exist. The statistics from most recent research indicate that today, pastors and their families are high priority satanic targets in society.

* Object 1: Begins with understanding that a Kingdom position is a spiritual appointment. Kingdom leaders must pray without ceasing as Apostle Paul advises; study, meditate, and obey the call and develop spiritually. Romans 8:14 says, *"For as many as are led by the Spirit of God, they are the sons of God."*

Our new life as Kingdom citizens is to live according to Spiritual principles not what you feel or think but based on the

Word of God. Supernatural men become common men when they are arrested by *sight*, insulted by *feelings* (emotions), distracted by *thoughts* (imagination), and prompted to talk as a result of the two. Feelings and emotions incubate thoughts and imaginations, whereas words initiate.

Both the privilege and the problem is that whatever you initiate by your conversation is what you call into existence for your future! Satan's goal is to remove you from your Spirit-filled expectations to *carnal reasoning's* and demote you to *sight-filled dominance*. As Kingdom leaders, there are two realities in life; the one you see and the one God exists in.

An example is 1 Kings 17-19, Elijah's supernatural operation using *faith* systems says, *"And Elijah the Tishbite, of the inhabitants of Gilead, said to Ahab, As the Lord God of Israel lives, before whom I stand, there shall not be dew nor rain these years, except at my word. Then the word of the Lord came to him, saying, get away from here and turn eastward, and hide by the Brook Cherith, which flows into the Jordan. And it will be that you shall drink from the brook, and I have commanded the ravens to feed you there. So he went and did according to the word of the Lord, for he went and stayed by the Brook Cherith, which flows into the Jordan."* In this passage, God instructed the prophet to hide by the Brook Cherith.

First Kings 18:1 says, *"And it came to pass after many days that the word of the Lord came to Elijah, in the third year, saying, go, present yourself to Ahab, and I will send rain on the earth.*" It does not appear that the increase in the provision nor the raising of the child had caused him to be recognized at Zarephath. If it had, it's possible Ahab would have discovered him. But in this chapter, his appearance was as public as before his isolation. During the days appointed for his concealment (part of the judgment upon Israel), he had not commanded interview with Obadiah, one of Ahab's servants, by whom he sends notice to Ahab of his coming (v. 2–16).

Second, his interview was with Ahab, himself (v. 17–20). Third, his interview with all Israel at Mount Carmel, in order to have a public trial of the prophets between the Lord and Baal. I think it is most important to note for the sake of this lesson, Elijah's dependence on God through faith initiated the supernatural which made two clear distinctions:

1. Baal and his prophets were confounded and executed. (v. 40)
2. God and Elijah were honored (v. 21–39). Afterward, mercy led to the return of rain accomplished by the word of *Elijah* (v. 41–46).

James 5:17-18, confirm Elijah's example is a direct result of *grace* initiated through *faith* by the spiritual tool; *effectual prayer. "Elijah was a man of like passion as we are. "And he prayed earnestly that it might not rain, and it did not rain on the earth for the time of three years and six months. And he prayed again, and the heaven gave rain, and the earth caused its fruit to sprout. "*

These passages demonstrate that Elijah's success was the result of the power of prayer. This should encourage us as kingdom leaders even in common cases, especially, if we consider that Elijah was a man of our like passions. He was zealous and a great man according to both history and the account of Apostle James. But like us, he had infirmities and was also subject to similar problems and disturbances from his passions; as are we. In prayer, we must not look to the merits of man, but to the grace of God. Only in this, should we imitate Elijah; how he prayed earnestly or as it is in the original; in prayer, he prayed. It is not enough to say a prayer, but we must *"pray in prayer!"*

Our thoughts must be fixed, our desires–*firm* and *ardent*, our graces in *exercise.* Elijah prayed that it might not rain, and it didn't for the span of three years and six months. Again he prayed, and the heavens gave rain. In 1 Kings 19:1-10, *"And Ahab told Jezebel all that Elijah had done, also how he had executed all the prophets with the sword. Then Jezebel sent a messenger to Elijah, saying, so let the gods do to me, and more also, if I do not make your life as the life of one of them by tomorrow about this time.*

And when he saw that, he arose and ran for his life, and went to Beersheba, which belongs to Judah, and left his servant there. But he himself went a day's journey into the wilderness, and came and sat down under a broom tree. And he prayed that he might die, and said, it is enough! Now, Lord, take my life, for I am no better than my fathers!" A prayer outside of the will of God that prompted no merit.

Then as he lay and slept under a broom tree, suddenly

an angel touched him, and said to him, Arise and eat. Then he looked, and there by his head was a cake baked on coals, and a jar of water. So he ate and drank, and lay down again. And the angel of the Lord came back the second time, and touched him, and said, Arise and eat, because the journey is too great for you. So he arose, and ate and drank; and he went in the strength of that food forty days and forty nights as far as Horeb, the mountain of God.

And there he went into a cave, and spent the night in that place; and behold, the word of the Lord came to him, and He said to him, 'What are you doing here, Elijah?' So he said, I have been very zealous for the Lord God of hosts; for the children of Israel have forsaken Your covenant, torn down Your altars, and killed Your prophets with the sword. I alone am left; and they seek to take my life."

By now, it must have been clear that man is more than what he sees because there is more to man than what meets the natural eye. He is a spirit that has a soul, which lives in a body. Since we are spirit-beings first, we must recognize the need to develop our spirit man first (John 6:63). I'm sure you know several Believers who have spent countless time and energy trying to bring their bodies in submission to God's way. They fail to understand that the natural man or body is the only part of our triune man at death that will be shed as the spirit and soul returns back to God.

Too many Believers focus the majority of their time, energy, and resources on natural pursuits and comforts. Rather than focusing their resources on spiritual development and submission to the Kingdom of God and His righteousness.

Setting Yourself in Order

There are *three* steps to properly establish priorities of the triune man. First, the natural man (body) or *sarkinoi* must be forced into submission. Second, the mind (soul) or *psyche* must be renewed and the affections set on things above. Third, the heart (spirit) or *pneuma* must be established and allowed to function as the chief of the three-part man. Successfully completing these three critical steps allow the *tri-une* to function properly. So, why are you waiting? You are only *three steps* away from structure!

Force the Natural Into Submission

Romans 8.8 implies, that to live according to the flesh is to live a life dominated by the dictates and desires of a sinful human nature. The flesh here is referred to as man's lower nature (his body or natural mind influenced by satanic and worldly advice). Notice, *flesh* cannot please God. *"So then they that are in the flesh cannot please God. But you are not in the flesh, but in the Spirit, if so be that the Spirit of God dwell in you."*

This is a very emphatic statement, factoring in a Believer's ability to experience prosperity in the Kingdom of God. Since this is the case at hand, Paul insists that a life dominated by such leaves a person vulnerable to the works of the flesh mentioned in Galatians 5:19-21. Declaring that "...*they which do such things shall not inherit the Kingdom of God.*" Each passage outlines the necessity of body subjection.

In Paul's first letter to Corinth, he explains the importance of bringing the body into compliance with God's Word to be worthy of receiving the prize. "*Know ye not that they which run in a race run all, but one receiveth the prize? So run, that ye may obtain. And every man that striveth for the mastery is temperate in all things. Now they do it to obtain a corruptible crown; but we are incorruptible. I, therefore so run, not as uncertainly; so fight I, not as one that beateth the air: But I keep under my body, and bring it into subjection: lest that by any means, when I have preached to others, I myself should be a castaway.*" (1 Corinthians 9.24-27, *KJV*)

Paul compares himself to the racers and combatants in the games well known to the Corinthians. Those who ran in their games were placed on a strict diet and had to exercise extreme discipline. In Paul's mind, they are the examples of how leaders and Believers should likewise abstain from fleshly appetites and heathenistic sacrifices for the heavenly crown. Those who fought with one another in these exercises prepared themselves by beating the air, as the Apostle calls it, or by throwing out their arms and thereby injuring themselves beforehand to better prepare themselves for close combat.

There is no room for any such exercise in Christian warfare. Christians are always in close combat. Our fleshly enemies make fierce and hearty opposition and are in constant pursuit of our bondage. Believers must remain earnest and never drop out of the contest, nor attempt to retire from it. We must fight, not as those who beat the air but strive against the strongholds with all our might. Paul mentions one contemptible enemy; the body (or the natural man). The body must be kept under, beaten black and blue (as the combatants were in the Grecian games) and constantly brought into subjection. By the "*body*," Paul is speaking of fleshly appetites and inclinations. Everyone who pursues their soul's interest must be committed to beat their bodies into compliance.

They must endure hard combat against fleshly lusts until they are subdued. The body must be made to serve the mind as it is renewed by spiritual principles and not be allowed for a moment to lord over it. For many years this was a difficult *truth* for me because like others, I thought there were still *good things* in my flesh.

Renew the mind and set affections on 'high things'

In other words, a person's thoughts should be tried and their feelings weighed because of potential deceptions from both. When a person becomes a Believer, he or she does not instantly think *godly* or *right*. Entry into any new arena or phase of life requires proper orientation. This is true in relationships, cultural changes, professions, career paths, new equipment and upgrades in technology.

This process has certainly been neglected in Christianity far too long. If industries and corporations understand the significance of employee orientation and training before allowing new employees to operate, the Body of Christ should at least realize that new converts must be oriented and trained as well. Next, kingdom leaders must remove *biased* leading methods and habits from kingdom positions and assignments even though it is not an easy task, largely because we have our hearts to contend with.

To be *biased* is to have a tendency or inclination about a specific thing. Especially one preventing *un*prejudiced consideration. Simply put—*to be prejudiced.* One of the greatest challenges facing the 21st-Century kingdom leader is: *Can you shrink enough to hear your overseer's heart without the need to get respect based on what you feel or think?*

Today's church needs *efficient* leaders. To be *efficient* is to function in the best possible manner with the *least* amount of time and effort invested. It is having and using necessary knowledge, skill, and resources to get the job done. Additionally, to be competent, capable, and reliable as an efficient operative. Consider the fact that, many times our *carnal reasoning* (inner dialogue) is stronger than the *spiritual voice* of God in our lives. So, we suffer not knowing the correct way to *view* things that only God can clarify.

Most men are like Nicodemus in John chapter three, who's view of himself was so distorted by his religion and his worldview that he could not understand Jesus' words. His perception was the offspring of his inner dialogue which was framed by reasoning *without* God's Word. When God said through Isaiah the prophet, "*My ways and thoughts are not the same as yours…*" notice He stated that we must *forsake* ours and *esteem* His "Word." Highly necessary to bridge the gulf.

CHAPTER 8
EXPOSITION OF OBJECTS

A Spiritual Leader must lead by <u>vision</u> which clarifies
the plans and missions of the ministry
(Proverbs 22:18; Habakkuk 2:2-4; Matthew 7:24-27)

🖐 Object 2: Kingdom Assignment Demands Vision
(Right Perspective):
"Where there is no vision [no redemptive revelation from
God], the people perish; but he who keeps the law [of God,
which includes that of man]–blessed (happy, fortunate, and
enviable) is he. Then the Lord told me: 'I will give you my
message in the form of a vision. Write it clearly enough to be
read at a glance. At the time I have decided, my words will
come true. You can trust what I say about the future. It may
take a long time, but keep on waiting— it will happen!" (CEV)
By combining each passage, it is clear that a kingdom or
spiritual assignment demands *vision*, or it may never surface

in the physical realm. Visionaries are leaders who have a crystal-clear picture in their minds of what is to happen. They cast visions powerfully and possess the indefatigable (untiring) enthusiasm to pursue their mission. Visionaries shamelessly appeal to anyone and everyone to get on board with their vision. They talk about it and write about it. They are *future-oriented*, usually idealistic, and full of faith to believe the vision can and will be actualized if the dream is talked about and cast often enough.

Visionary leaders are not easily discouraged or deterred. In fact, if people tell them their dream is impossible, it simply adds fuel to the fire within their spirit. Visionary leaders may or may not form teams, align talents, set goals, or manage progress toward the achievement of the vision. But this one thing is sure; *they carry the vision*. They cast the vision. They draw people into the vision, and they'll die seeing it to fruition.

Clearly the emphasis of Proverbs 29:18 suggests that any person, family, group, organization, government system, or society that is without "*vision*" is destined to perish. This makes seeing and perceiving the *vision* essential for every leader. Visions must serve as the internal filtration device leaders use to make pertinent decisions, determine priorities, establish activities and duties, and respond to all shifting circumstances and unanticipated challenges on a regular basis.

As a Leader, the vision must act as a default mechanism that enables consistent decisions that impact the flow of your life and ability to continue mounting progress. In other words, *visions* help determine the persons, activities, habits, environments, rests, diets and other significant functions that should be a part of your life. This is why I refer to visions as the *cornerstone* of a prosperous life. Webster's New World Dictionary defines it as: The basic, essential, or most important part of a foundation.

From it, all the necessary components are drafted. I often quote, "He who fails to *plan, plans* to fail!" I see so much potential wasted daily as a pastor. Especially in the lives of resourceful people who just don't know how to tap into their essence.

The plan

Planning is an overlooked *life* principle. Proverbs 16:1,3,9 says,

"The preparations of the heart in man, and the answer of the tongue, is from the Lord."

"Commit thy works unto the Lord, and thy thoughts shall be established."

"A man's heart plans his way: but the Lord directs his steps."

This means, *we plan* the way we want to live, but only *God makes* us able to live it. Kingdom life for a kingdom man begins with a kingdom plan. In fact, many fail to understand that the divine key to leadership, headship, managing life, directing a marriage, raising children, and maintaining a quality life is a strong plan. Many women and a majority of wives are frustrated because the men in their lives have no plan for their family.

Brothers, if you desire a quality life, it begins with a *quality* kingdom plan. Think about it, without a quality plan and purpose what reason does the Holy Spirit have to speak to you? What would He guide you to do if it fulfills no plan? Look at these words of wisdom, "Without a *vision*, people perish?" In other words, continue to live in defeat and frustration because life awaits their vision application which commands a response. Notice that God tries to convince us that we all have purpose, and that He, Himself planned our existence upon Earth.

In Jeremiah 29:11 God says, *"For I know the thoughts that I think toward you, saith the Lord, thoughts of peace, and not of evil, to give you hope in your latter end."* This is God's promise, even though it seems life constantly challenges you with one test or another. This is when you take charge over your existence. God has given you His Son, His Word, His Spirit, His promise, and His pastors. (Ephesians 1:3, 2: 1 Peter 1:3) As kingdom leaders, you must take dominion over and manage your time, circumstances, and expectations.

Today, put a *plan* in place that demands your life conforms to the *expectations and desires God planted inside you before birth*. To put it in simple terms; we cannot enter into *realities* we cannot *see* within ourselves.

I often remind the congregation I shepherd, that impatience will cause you to forfeit your righteous expectations of faith, and if you're not careful you will return to your old frustrating habits instead of trusting God's way.

Today, realize that *if* you had taken the time years ago to develop a plan with God's assistance, the majority of your decisions, actions, and habits would correspond with your preplanned and well-organized expectations. Hebrews 10:36 says, *"For you have need of steadfast patience and endurance, so that after you have done the will of God, you may receive and enjoy to the full benefit of what God has promised."* But it's hard to be *patient* without a *plan* when you don't know what to *expect* next. This corresponds with Habakkuk 2:2-4. Meditate on these passages. You are closer to establishing your heart in the righteousness of faith beliefs. Establishing your heart is the first phase to constant kingdom manifestations.

What's the *plan*?

Behind the veil of many successful *financial* relationships with God is an untold *truth*, not rehearsed enough in the corridors of religion. A *plan.* A plan is not only a *lifeline* but also a specific receiving device for priority decisions made regarding selections for *all* inclusions to one's destiny. It serves as a navigation device and a *filtration* device for critical decisions and future forecast to determine expectations that correspond with one's purpose. It is an *accountability* measure that can be used to keep an individual within a certain scope and parameter for operation and actions.

Visions written: Plans declare your readiness for success

In the past, having no goals, either large or small, seemed an exercise in foolishness since I had so little *faith* in my abilities. Each day, I would stumble out into the world hoping to survive until sunset without a plan. I learned that to drift from day-to-day is easy. No skill required, nor pain or effort. On the other hand, to set goals for a day, a week, or a month and attain those objectives is never easy.

Tomorrow, I will begin. This is what I told myself day-after-day. I did not know then, that tomorrow is only found in the calendars of fools. Blind to my foolish faults, I wasted my life in deliberation. I procrastinated until it was too late but had it not been for this spiritual awakening, I learned that there is an immeasurable distance between late and too late.

Those who subject themselves to this type of living are in a fool's alley. To always intend on making a new and better life but never to find time to get to it, is as if I should put off eating and drinking and sleeping from one day to the next until I'm dead. For too many years, I was convinced, like so many others, that the only worthwhile goals were priceless goals with the rich rewards of gold, fame, and power. But now I know that wise men never make goals of massive proportions.

Those plans that are giant in size, called dreams and are cradled close to the heart where others may not see and mock them. Then he greets each morning with goals for the day only, and make certain that all he plans is completed before he sleeps. Soon, the accomplishments of each day are gathered, one atop another, likened to ant piles his grains of sand, and eventually, a castle is erected large enough to house his dream. I call this the art of learning to harness my impatience and deal with life one day at a time.

"The victory of success is half won when one gains the habit of setting goals and achieving them."
(Og Mandino)

Exposition of Objects: Object interval

Without faith, vision is unsustainable and has no substance.

Proverbs 29:18 (*AMP*) says,

"Where there is no vision [no redemptive revelation of God], the people perish; but he who keeps the law [of God, which includes that of man]–blessed (happy, fortunate, and enviable) is he." (1 Samuel 3:1; Amos 8:11, 12)

"But without faith, it is impossible to please and be satisfactory to Him. For whoever would come near to God must [necessarily] believe that God exists and that He is the rewarder of those who earnestly and diligently seek Him [out]." (Hebrews 11:6, *AMP*)

Vision generates hope, faith sustains hope. Hope is an invisible quality that is indistinguishable without a word or an image. Once a word is spoken, or an image conceived, hope initiates the will to pursue its reality. Paul says in

111

Romans 8:24-25, *"For we are saved by hope: but hope that is seen is not hope: for what a man seeth, why doth he yet hope for? But if we hope for that we see not, then do we with patience wait for it."*

The Amplified says, *"For in [this] hope we were saved. But hope [the object of] which is seen is not hope. For how can one hope for what he already sees? But if we hope for what is still unseen by us, we wait for it with patience and composure."*

Here faith sustains hope until patience allows it to become material reality. This is why, Romans 8:26 (*NKJV*), says *"Likewise the Spirit also helps in our weaknesses."* That weakness is your inability to intellectualize your need conceptually. *"For we do not know what we should pray for as we ought."* (our intellect is not yet developed) but the Spirit Himself makes intercession for us with groanings which cannot be uttered."

Vision is the mind of God planted in the mind of man for the sake of accomplishing God's plan and purpose for their life. If faith is the substance of the thing we hope for, then vision must make that substance believable reality until we gain concept for *how to* bring it into natural reality.

Faith is the force and function of God in all aspects of the kingdom. The Kingdom of God does not exist initially in the natural, physical realm because the first manifestation of the Kingdom of God is in the Spiritual, heavenly realm. It is *invisible first!* This means to have Faith without vision is blind faith. Faith is the actual substance, but the *vision is the descriptive image or picture of that substance which makes it tangible to mental sight for the concept.*

In the natural realm, the senses make all natural things tangible for concept and relativity.

Likewise, faith and vision combined makes all spiritual things tangible for concept and relativity. The mind houses spiritual sight which reflects the vision that comes from hope generated by the *words of faith.*

To further explain let's look at John 18: 35, 36. *"Pilate answered, 'Am I a Jew? Your own nation and the chief priests have delivered you to me. What have you done?'"*

Jesus answered, *"My kingdom is not of this world. If My kingdom were of this world, my servants would fight, so that I should not be delivered to the Jews; but now My Kingdom is not from here."*

In other words, my *Kingdom* is not of the physical world because the kingdom of God is of a spiritual essence [spiritual things are discerned]. (1 Corinthians 2:14) Here, faith must become to the spirit-man, what physical eyes are to the natural man. The things that govern spiritual, or invisible life are all based in a spiritual environment. This is why we are encouraged in Ephesians 6:10-12 to *"...be strong in the Lord, and in the power of his might. Put on the whole armor of God, that ye may be able to stand against the wiles of the devil. For we wrestle not against flesh and blood, but against principalities, against powers, against the rulers of the darkness of this world, against spiritual wickedness in high places."*

As *kingdom leaders,* remember that your mind is what the devil fights through your senses to keep you distracted from kingdom purpose. He wants to *blind your mind!* For many leaders, mind-blindness is a mind preoccupied with non-essential things. In other words, he gives you something more desirable but least in priority to think about.

♦ Object 3: *Right Activity* (Faith)

Jehoshaphat feared, Samuel almost anointed the wrong son, and Moses sent twelve spies and ten returned with a bad report and all but two of them died in the wilderness. Faith has two enemies; fear and doubt. This is caused by incorrect belief systems. Incorrect *belief* has one ally, unconfirmed knowledge. Unconfirmed knowledge has one ally; *ignorance!* Ignorance has one major ally; the *habit* of acting without instruction.

What does it really mean for a kingdom leader to walk and live by faith daily? How important is it for kingdom leaders to make faith their only option for leading God's people? In the Kingdom of God's system there is an interchangeable, overlapping quality associated with all life and relationships that govern principles. Faith, which is the function of God, is to be seen as the covering for all exchanges in righteousness. The first component of the righteousness of God, is faith. (Galatians 2:16)

Everything the kingdom leader does should be done by, in, and through faith. When we fail to exchange by faith, our conversations, judgments, confrontations, adversities and favors are responses from our lower nature. Whatever isn't grounded in faith is *sin*. This is important because whatever we think consciously influences the direction, quality, and present state of our lives. To Walk by faith requires the leaders' conscious mind, thoughts, and pondering according to the Word of God instead of the dictation and suggestions of natural sight and sensual perceptions.

Another reason is, whatever I say to myself repetitiously influences angels or demons; the forces of the spiritual realm. So I must watch what I say to myself. Ecclesiastes 5:2 says, *"Do not be quick with your mouth, do not be hasty in your heart to utter anything before God. God is in heaven and you are on earth, so let your words be few." (NIV) The Good News Translation* says, *"Think before you speak, and don't make any rash promises to God. He is in heaven and you are on earth, so don't say any more than you have to."*

This is important because Satan enjoys conversing with us all the time to get us saying things to ourselves that he wants to bring into our reality. He understands that our worlds are framed by words. We are so accustomed to him speaking to us through our carnal thinking and reasoning, that most don't consider the words being exchanged. Like he attempted to do with Jesus in the wilderness. Notice he said to Jesus, *"if You are the Son of God, command these stones to bread."*

In the first test, Jesus knew to say only what God's Word says because he knew that God's Word automatically rebukes the devil. The second test he presented Jesus was the same test he presented Eve in the garden. He hoped to trick Jesus into rebellion as an act of His faith. Satan told Jesus, "The Scripture says, *'He has given His angels charge over you'* *and won't let anything happen to you.'"* But, the truth is that he wanted Jesus to act out of presumption rather than faith initiated by the will of God.

How many times has the devil succeeded in Christian leaders' lives? How many have said before, "I *feel* that God is leading me another way." simply because they are offended? However, when you ask why they aren't in fellowship and fulfilling their position or why they aren't obeying Scripture in handling their offense, I've heard things such as, "God hasn't revealed what to do yet."

The kingdom leader must realize the first component of God's righteousness is faith, which is the reason Hebrews 11:6 says, *"Without faith it is impossible to please God."* Even though the kingdom leader is constantly buffeted with many challenges, he must remain in faith or chance losing his spiritual composure. Paul said in 2 Corinthians 4:8-10 and 12-14,

"We are hard-pressed on every side, yet not crushed; we are perplexed, but not in despair; persecuted, but not forsaken; struck down, but not destroyed— always carrying about in the body the dying of the Lord Jesus, that the life of Jesus also may be manifested in our body."

This means that death works in us but life also works in

us. In the Scriptures it says, *"I spoke because I had faith."* We have this same kind of faith. So we speak because we know that God raised the Lord Jesus to Life. Just as God raised Jesus, he will also raise us to life. Then, He will bring us into His presence together. In this, God's Word or the word of faith gives specific principle details concerning how to righteously handle challenges, indifference, adversity, and offenses. Regardless of the situation or who it consists of, the word of faith must be the *final authority*.

Without obedience to the Word of God, the leader's behavior is exposed and viewed as rebellion to kingdom authority. Which invites unpredictable consequences upon the leader that could have been avoided. Romans 10:6-9 says, *"But the righteousness of faith speaks this way, "Do not say in your heart, 'who will ascend into heaven?'"* (that is, to bring Christ down from above). Or who will descend into the abyss? (that is, to bring Christ up from the dead). But what does it say? "The word is near you, in your mouth and in your heart (that is, the word of faith which we preach): that if you confess with your mouth the Lord Jesus and believe in your heart that God has raised Him from the dead, you will be saved."

The first component of faith is the Word of God, which is the source from God that directs, substantiates, governs, and establishes the Believer's hope and trust in God. Again, Romans 10:8, 9 says, *"The word is near you, in your mouth and in your heart"* (the word of faith which we preach). If you confess with your mouth the Lord Jesus and believe in your heart that God has raised Him from the dead, you will be saved.

In John 15:7,8 Jesus said, "If you abide in Me, and My words abide in you, you will ask what you desire, and it shall be done for you. By this My Father is glorified, that you bear much fruit; so you will be My disciples." The implications are that this conscious abiding displays the discipline that glorifies God and makes the kingdom citizen fruitful. This conscious readiness displays a continual walk in faith which prepares an individual to rely on and trust in God's way.

Habakkuk 2:2-4, Romans 1:16, Galatians 3 and Hebrews 10 says, the just, declared, or uncompromisingly righteous shall live by faith. The kingdom leader must know at all times how to locate his faith in the midst of test and trials. In Luke's account the winds and the waves obey Jesus, but the disciples could not locate their faith.

Luke 8:22-25 further says, *"Now it happened, on a certain day, that He got into a boat with His disciples. And He said to them, 'Let us cross over to the other side of the lake.' And they launched out. But as they sailed He fell asleep. And a windstorm came down on the lake, and they were filling with water, and were in jeopardy. And they came to Him and awoke Him, saying, 'Master, Master, we are perishing!' Then He arose and rebuked the wind and the raging of the water. And they ceased, and there was a calm. But He said to them, 'Where is your faith?' And they were afraid, and marveled, saying to one another, 'Who can this be? For He commands even the winds and water, and they obey Him!'"* (*NKJV*)

It is important to note that after Jesus calmed the storm, He then, gives them a rebuke for their inordinate fear: Where is your faith? (Luke 8:25) In that they were afraid, and marveled, they exposed their failure to comply with the demands of living and walking by faith as a kingdom principle. Some leaders proclaim to have true faith have to seek it or, for neglect or lack of practice, cannot locate it when they have occasion or opportunity to use it.

Like the disciples, they tremble, and are discouraged, allowing little things to dishearten them. Here, Jesus as their teacher conveys by experience the importance of staying in faith. Leaders must remember their words convey the abundance of their heart and in times of testing must prove as the psalmist says, *"He will not be afraid of evil tidings; His heart is steadfast, trusting in the LORD."* His heart is established; He will not be afraid, until he sees his desire upon his enemies. (Psalms 112:7, 8, *NKJV*)

In the midst of our challenges stay poised, practiced, and well prepared to face multiple oppositions and adversaries. Let's look briefly at what faith is and how Jesus said it must be regarded and acted on in order to advance the leader as a Kingdom citizen. First, know that the kingdom assignment and position always requires and demands faith in everything, at all times.

Everything 'faith'

To begin, let's establish that the Law of Faith is activated by repentance, affirmed by obedience, comes by hearing, and begins where the will of God is known and appropriated. Romans 10:17 confirms the source of faith comes by hearing the Word of God. This is what Jesus implied when stating *"It has been written, Man shall not live and be upheld and sustained by bread alone, but by every word that comes forth from the mouth of God."* (Matthew 4:4)

Romans 12:3 is clear that God has dealt to every man the measure of faith. Galatians 5:22 reveals the fruit of faith provides character. The word of faith in Romans 10:8 is for nourishment.

In Hebrews 4:1-2 the apostle made it clear that the word of faith is profitable to us only when or if we mix what we hear with faith. "Therefore, since a promise remains of entering His rest, let us fear lest any of you seem to have come short of it. For indeed the gospel was preached to us as well as to them; but the Word which they heard did not profit them, not being mixed with faith in those who heard it. The Law of Faith mentioned in Romans 3:27 is for the regulation of the new life of the kingdom citizen, the gift of faith in 1 Corinthians 12:9 is given to us for the supernatural, and the Spirit of Faith in 2 Corinthians 4:13 provides fervency through belief and speech.

Notice how it is stated, "And since we have the same spirit of faith, according to what is written, "I believed and therefore I spoke," we also believe and therefore speak, implying the importance of our duplication of His methods. The multiple and diverse results of faith in Hebrews eleven gives us illustrated proof of the broadness of the functional operation of faith. It also demonstrates the importance of its inclusion in all our affairs and exchanges when it is employed to assist and serve us in every situation. Clearly, the kingdom leader must know that "Whatsoever is not of *faith* is sin."

Mark 8:13-21 says, "And he left them, and again entering into the boat departed to the other side. And they forgot to take bread; and they had not in the boat with them more than one loaf. And he charged them, saying, Take heed, beware of the leaven of the Pharisees and the leaven of Herod. And they reasoned one with another, saying, We have no bread. And Jesus perceiving it saith unto them, Why reason ye, because ye have no bread? do ye not yet perceive, neither understand? have ye your heart hardened? Having eyes, see ye not? and having ears, hear ye not? and do you not remember?

When I brake the five loaves among the five thousand, how many baskets full of broken pieces took ye up? They say unto him, twelve. And when the seven among the four thousand, how many basketfuls of broken pieces took ye up? And they say unto him, seven. And he said unto them, Do ye not yet understand?" (*ASV*) He wanted them to understand that their lives demanded faith, 24/7. Not some situations in, others out. Or, some exchanges faith, others carnal reasoning's. The kingdom leader must always, in all things, walk by faith or their position will become perplexed.

Life in the kingdom requires constant learning, open-mindedness, and a commitment to hearing and receiving wise instructions in keeping with the lifestyle of faith. "All Scripture is given by inspiration of God, and is profitable for doctrine, for reproof, for correction, for instruction in righteousness, that the man of God may be complete, thoroughly equipped for every good work." (2 Timothy 3:16, 17, *NKJV*)

The kingdom leader's words

Hebrews 11:3, *"By faith we understand that the worlds were framed by the word of God, so that the things which are seen were not made of things which are visible."* (*NKJV*) The Amplified says it this way, *"By faith we understand that the worlds [during the successive ages] were framed (fashioned, put in order, and equipped for their intended purpose) by the Word of God, so that what we see was not made out of things which are visible."* (Also John 1:1-3 and Joshua 1:8)

Since words of faith are vital for the Kingdom Leader to establish the proper application of Grace. Here are three questions that will assist you in daily growth and effective kingdom living.

1. Are your words influencing godliness in you?
2. Do you consider the source and intention of your words before you release them?

3. Have you developed the habit of releasing your words to promote God's blessings and favor in the lives of yourself and others?

Notice, Matthew 21:18-22:

"Now in the morning, as He (the leader) returned to the city, He was hungry. And seeing a fig tree by the road, He came to it and found nothing on it but leaves, and said to it, "Let no fruit grow on you ever again." Immediately the fig tree withered away. And when the disciples (the followers) saw it, they marveled, saying, "How did the fig tree wither away so soon?" (*NKJV*)

So Jesus (the leader) answered and said to them, "Assuredly, I say to you, if you have faith and do not doubt, you will not only do what was done to the fig tree, but also if you say to this mountain, 'Be removed and be cast into the sea,' it will be done. And whatever things you ask in prayer, believing, you will receive."

In this example *Jesus* demonstrated the power and the importance of releasing words of faith to influence the response of natural things in the life of a kingdom leader. I call this a thermostat state of mind because faith is greater force than sight. When a leader's mindset is thermostatic, he's looking to *set* the tone, or mood of the environment rather than allow ungodliness or wickedness to establish moods and behaviors which demand conformance.

Some leaders are active and assertive, while others are passive and inactive. Passivity never pays off. God will match our effort, but He will never do our work for us. This is why He gave us the *measure* of faith. It is to serve us, or serve God's interest in our lives. God's grace will cover our failures, but it will not make up for our passivity. We have to do our part. I once knew a near eighty-year-old mother who spoke negative about everything she was a part of every day of her life. Her family, job, home conditions, children, her health—*everything*.

One day, I received a call that she was sick and the doctor had summoned the family to her bedside and given her a short time to live. I was also told that she requested I come. So I made my way there expeditiously. After I arrived, it was clear that she wasn't ready to let go, so I asked her to commit to speak only words of faith as I prayed for her. She replied, *"Well it must be God's will because it seems like I've been hurting and sick all my life. Just can't get better like some of the rest of 'em."* I really wanted to tell her that ever since I'd known her, from each greeting throughout my entire visit, she only spoke negative about everything. Her words were corrupting her heart and therefore had affected her life.

I said, "Sweetheart you've gotta change the way you speak about things in order to overcome this condition. The power of God is present to heal, but you've got to be willing to believe and trust Him. Your words of Faith will be an asset to the development and continued confidence of your trusting God to heal and deliver you." She said, "Well, maybe if you'll just stay here with me a while, I'll get better."

As I began to pray for her, after about an hour, standing by her bedside, I could sense that she was slipping away. Her last words to me were, "*I think I see my mamma and son beckoning for me, so it won't be long now.*" Suddenly I could sense the peace of God, so I held her hand until she took her last breath.

Although this beautiful mother did not attend my sanctuary for worship not Bible Study, she did believe in me as a leader. An even though she never changed her speech, the conversations we had around her bed, greatly impacted her family and influenced several of her children and grands to receive Christ as their Savior and change their speech. This is important because Ephesians 4:29-32 AMP, warns, "Let no foul or polluting language, nor evil word nor unwholesome or worthless talk [ever] come out of your mouth, but only such [speech] as is good and beneficial to the spiritual progress of others, as is fitting to the need and the occasion, that it may be a blessing and give *grace* (God's favor) to those who hear it.

And do not grieve the Holy Spirit of God [do not offend or vex or sadden Him], by whom you were sealed (marked, branded as God's own, secured) for the day of redemption (of final deliverance through Christ from evil and the consequences of sin). Let all bitterness and indignation and wrath (passion, rage, bad temper) and resentment (anger, animosity) and quarreling (brawling, clamor, contention) and slander (evil-speaking, abusive or blasphemous language) be banished from you, with all malice (spite, ill will, or baseness of any kind).

And become useful and helpful and kind to one another, tenderhearted (compassionate, understanding, loving-hearted), forgiving one another [readily and freely], as God in Christ forgave you."

Now that we've clarified the importance of correct speech and the kingdom leaders use of Right Words to initiate righteous exchanges. Let's identify the correct way a leader is to consistently function and effect the continual growth of God's people. Also, how to avoid false expectations between leadership and the congregation.

Matthew 6:31-33 says, "Therefore do not worry, saying, 'What shall we eat?' or 'What shall we drink?' or 'What shall we wear?'

For after all these things the Gentiles seek. For your heavenly father knows that you need all these things.

But seek first the Kingdom of God and His righteousness, and all these things shall be added to you.

In other words, *seek* to identify and distinguish exactly how God handles His affairs before proceeding. The pursuit of righteous instructions is supposed to put the kingdom leader in a posture of confident expectations rather than worry and fear. These three verses in context, implies that when the Believer or kingdom leader puts seeking God's Kingdom and Righteousness first, the things that Gentiles build their lives around as a pursuit, are simply added.

In this a kingdom-first mindset, which equals new life of addition through a covenant partnership with Christ the anointed and all the heavenly host in the invisible realm. My emphasis from this perspective is to teach the importance of walking in the 'now' tense of faith which comes from faith in the finished work of Christ! But, even in this, every Believer, especially, kingdom leaders must know and understand that the strength of your spirit does not void out the vulnerability of the soul, nor, the gullibility of the body.

As Sons of men who are born-again, the reason we as leaders must exercise ourselves in God's righteousness, which is the righteousness of faith, is because everyday accounts for itself, and God's righteousness requires of us, a different approach to our way of acting and performing in His affairs. Since the "kingdom is always under assault," the leader must be committed; suited and equipped for warfare at all times, which requires right alignment. The kingdom leader who fails to stay in faith will cease to reflect or represent God's way of righteousness before His sheep.

Ultimately, the leader becomes responsible for the compounding assumption that a religious effort is sufficient. This behavior diminishes the strength of God's Word making the commandments of men more impressionable than the righteousness of faith. Refer to my book: *Imposing your Faith* for further clarity.

 Object 4: *Love* (Right Motive)

Kingdom faith works by love. In spiritual matters, faith

needs vision or its blind-faith. Faith must also be motivated by love to make it profitable for all kingdom service and to make the servant a representative of God.

"But *faith* works by *love*." Matthew 5:43-46 (*AMP*)

"You have heard that it was said, you shall love your neighbor and hate your enemy; (Leviticus 19:18; Psalm 139:21, 22) But I tell you, love your enemies and pray for those who persecute you. (Proverbs 25:21, 22) "To show that you are the children of your Father who is in heaven; for He makes His sun rise on the wicked and on the good, and makes the rain fall upon the upright and the wrongdoers [alike]. For if you love those who love you, what reward can you have? Do not even the tax collectors do that?"

Mark 12:28-34 (ASV) "And one of the scribes came, and heard them questioning together, and knowing that he had answered them well, asked him, What commandment is the first of all? Jesus answered, the first is, hear, O Israel; The Lord our God and the Lord are one: and thou shalt love the Lord thy God with all thy heart, and with all thy soul, and with all thy mind, and with all thy strength. The second is this, thou shalt love thy neighbor as thyself. There is no other commandment greater than these."

"And the scribe said unto him, of a truth, teacher, thou hast well said that he is one; and there is none other but he: and to love him with all the heart, and with all the understanding, and with all the strength, and to love his neighbor as himself, is much more than all whole burnt-offerings and sacrifices.

And when Jesus saw that he answered discreetly, he said unto him, Thou art not far from the kingdom of God. And no man after that durst ask him any question."

In this illustration Jesus makes it clear, that even though, 'without faith it's impossible to please God.' Love is essential because it is the very nature and essence of God. Therefore, without love, faith is not reflective of God. As you journey, keep in mind, leadership is a 'people business' and kingdom leadership is a 'people business' that requires a godly *love* for those who are to be affected by your position, influence, and service.

It was the *love* of God that started this redemption principle and process from the beginning. For God so loved the world, that *He gave* his only begotten Son, that whosoever believeth on Him should not perish, but have eternal life. (John 3:16) Since it is clear that leadership is a people business, the purpose of leadership is to produce leaders, not followers. Jesus said, "He that will be great among you shall be your servant." To be great you have to serve others. The more people you serve the greater you become.

Dr. Myles Munroe says there are three necessary attributes to becoming a great leader:
1. A belief in one's self. He said, "All true leaders have an affair with themselves because they believe in themselves so much they don't need your encouragement. This makes them very dangerous. Additionally, he quoted Jesus' words in Mark chapter four: "those who do not

have root in themselves" can be shifted too easily by the opinions of others.

2. A *passion* for the job and not afraid to fail.

3. A love for people. Loving people requires knowing who you are and who they are. Jesus answered saying to them: "They that are in health have no need of a physician; but they that are sick. I am not come to call the righteous but sinners to repentance." (Luke 5:28-32, *ASV*) This love assumes its rightful position in the lives of others at all times. In the Kingdom of God system there is an interchangeable, overlapping quality associated with all life and relationship governing principles.

Faith, which is the force and function of God, is to be seen as the *covering* for all our exchanges in righteousness. Everything we do should be done by, in, or through "faith." When we fail to exchange by faith, all conversations, judgments, confrontations, adversities and favors, are responses from our lower nature, (whatever is not of faith is sin). In the kingdom system, faith is the activator, but, *love* is the motivator. Faith activates kingdom love and love motivates Godly faith. Which is empowered by the Holy Spirit to promote righteous exchanges that glorify God.

Having been justified by faith, we have peace with God through our Lord Jesus Christ, through whom also we have access by faith into this grace in which we stand and rejoice in hope of the glory of God. Even though faith as a principle covers us, love corrects us by cleansing our motives for righteous exchanges. Luke 6:41-42 (*ASV*) says, Jesus established the priority of love from the perspective of a strong and well-balanced person. *"And why beholdest thou the mote that is in thy brother's eye, but considerest not the beam that is in thine own eye? Or how canst thou say to thy brother, 'Brother, let me cast out the mote that is in thine eye,' when thou, thyself beholdest not the beam that is in thine own eye? Thou hypocrite, cast out first the beam from thine own eye, and then shalt thou see clearly to cast out the mote that is in thy brother's eye."*

A well-balanced person has three things:

- SELF- concept
- SELF- worth
- SELF- esteem

Scriptural references:

In this, Jesus made *love* the most important emotion and functional expression for all social exchanges. Matthew 18:35 (*NKJV*), *"So, my heavenly Father also will do to you if each of you, from his heart, does not forgive his brother his trespasses."* The implications are clear that God expects His leaders to have a constant heart-cleansing mindset to act from a position of love toward His people.

Many times the leader will discover that others in their assignment or on their team have problems that are being whispered instead of confronted and discussed to clarify. When this occurs, the wise leader seeks to deal with the adversity upon discovery, by prudent scriptural means as soon as possible. This keeps adversity, offense, and contrariness minimized so that the infections of leaven among brothers is not allowed.

Jesus said, "Offenses must come." First John 2:9-11 (*NKJV*), says, "*He who says he is in the light and hates his brother, is in darkness until now. He who loves his brother abides in the light, and there is no cause for stumbling in him. But he who hates his brother is in darkness and walks in darkness, and does not know where he is going, because the darkness has blinded his eyes.*"

The imperative of love is established in 1 John 3:10-15: "In this the children of God and the children of the devil are manifest: Whoever does not practice righteousness is not of God, nor is he who does not love his brother. For this is the message that you heard from the beginning, that we should love one another, not as Cain who was of the wicked one and murdered his brother. And why did he murder him? Because his works were evil and his brother's righteous.

Do not marvel, my brethren, if the world hates you. We know that we have passed from death to life, because we love the brethren.

He who does not love his brother abides in death. Whoever hates his brother is a murderer, and you know that no murderer has eternal life abiding in him." (*NKJV*) Next, John the apostle establishes the outworkings of love. "By this we know love, because He laid down His life for us. And we also ought to lay down our lives for the brethren. But whoever has this world's goods, and sees his brother in need, and shuts up his heart from him, how does the love of God abide in him? My little children, let us not love in word or in tongue, but in deed and in truth." (1 John 3:16-18, *NKJV*)

First John 4:16-20, 21 (*NKJV*), "And we have known and believed the love that God has for us. God is love, and he who abides in love abides in God, and God in him. If someone says, 'I love God,' and hates his brother, he is a liar; for he who does not love his brother whom he has seen, how can he love God whom he has not seen? And this commandment we have from Him: that he who loves God must love his brother also."

Paul, the apostle, also explains both the antithesis and the absolute importance of kingdom leaders having love as a right motive. First Corinthians 13:1-8, 13: "Though I speak with the tongues of men and of angels, but have not love, I have become a sounding brass or a clanging cymbal. And though I have the gift of prophecy, and understand all mysteries and all knowledge, and though I have all faith, so that I could remove mountains, but have not love, I am nothing. And though I bestow all my goods to feed the poor, and though I give my body to be burned, but have not love, it profits me nothing.

Love suffers long and is kind; love does not envy; love does not parade itself, is not puffed up; does not behave rudely, does not seek its own, is not provoked, thinks no evil; does not rejoice in iniquity, but rejoices in the truth; bears all things, believes all things, hopes all things, endures all things. Loe never fails. But whether there are prophecies, they will fail; whether there are tongues, they will cease; whether there is knowledge, it will vanish away. And now abide faith, hope, love, these three; but the greatest of these is *love.*" (*NKJV*)

LOVE is a most essential quality because it empowers us to live a self-less life that places no unnecessary demands on others in relationship to us. It is a godly love which ensures that we have right motives ourselves, first. Especially in that we are required to "*Love our neighbors as ourselves.*" Agape or divine love, frees us and makes us better able to embrace others genuinely, and become better equipped to serve their concerns without including our own selfish expectations or demands.

In order for the kingdom leader to consistently express agape requires the nine fruit sof the Spirit be practiced and nurtured within every kingdom leader to keep our hearts aligned for righteous exchanges. This is necessary because each time kingdom leaders fail to exchange or manifest spiritual fruit we fall short of interacting in the way that pleases or glorifies God. Let your light so shine before men, that they may see your good works and glorify your Father in heaven. (Matthew 5:16, *NKJV*) These nine fruit together house the *perfect love* which cast out all fears and becomes the charity that never fails. This allows others to know that we are Christ disciples because we love and serve one another by it.

On this impactful display of kingdom righteousness, the

Scripture says, "Hang all the prophets and the law." First John 4:7-11, 18 reveals God's expectations: "Beloved, let us love one another: for love is of God; and every one that loveth is born of God, and knoweth God. He that loveth not knoweth not God; for God is love. In this was manifested the love of God toward us, because that God sent his only begotten Son into the world, that we might live through him. Herein is love, not that we loved God, but that he loved us, and sent his Son to be the propitiation for our sins. (*KJV*)

Beloved, if God so loved us, we ought also to love one another. In verse 18, John emphasizes love as the solution to all relational insecurities and fears. "There is no fear in love; but perfect love casteth out fear: because fear hath torment. He that feareth is not made perfect in love." Galatians 5:14-16 says, "For all the law is fulfilled in one word, even in this; Thou shalt love thy neighbor as thyself. But if ye bite and devour one another, take heed that ye be not consumed one of another. This I say then, walk in the Spirit, and ye shall not fulfil the lust of the flesh."

Proverbs 10:12, 18-19 says, "Hatred stirs up strife; But love covers all transgressions.

He that hides hatred has lying lips; And he that utters or spreads slander is a fool. In the multitude of words there wanteth not transgression; But he that refrains his lips does wisely." Clearly the kingdom leader must be resolved to walk in love in order to demonstrate the character of God consistently.

CHAPTER 9
LEADERS. STAFF.
RELATIONSHIPS.

I pray that you will wisely consider and ponder some priceless information I learned from a leadership class with Dr. A.R. Barnard. He made the following statement: "There werc places and relationships in Jesus' life that the disciples were not familiar with, because He did not expose them to His most sacred quarters. There were also places that only a select few were permitted to go with him.

Principle: His approach to each of them was based upon their level of maturity. This means there were places only those most mature were allowed to go.

Point: All kingdom leaders must learn to manage their expectations, especially, with the staff.

Reason: In relationships, we live in tension between the *ideal*---and---*reality*.

This tension consist of how things ought to be, how

we want them to be, and how they really are. The distance between the ideal and the reality determines the level of disappointment we experience when something unfavorable occurs or when something adversely affects us relationally. Here, the primary reason the leader must be conscious of their staff's level of maturity is because what we expect from those under us *may not correspond* with their ability to perform as we desire or a position or task maybe simply too demanding for that person. In any case what's most important is that the staff member, after a thorough assessment, only be put in a position or environment in which they can succeed.

A leader is required to: Wisely judge staff to determine what place they should hold in the leadership circle, if any at all. They must be courageous enough to replace and make changes as are necessary. We live life on levels, which means some leaders cannot see or understand from your perspective. We arrive in stages, which makes it vitally important to qualify the person by using the three A's; accountability, accessibility, and ability. So as you move from one level to the next, the intimacy changes because everyone is not always moving in the same direction, at the same time as you.

In cases where a staff member fails to move in the same direction as their leader or fail to understand the leader's position, defer to one of the three Rs to manage them successfully:
1. Retrain them if they're receptive and desire to change by

growing to expand their capacity to fill the position.

2. Reposition by attempting to redeem them by assigning them to a lessor demand.

3. Retire the individual as soon as you discern or determine they've changed or shifted against your authority and judgement as the Senior Leader.

It takes courage to lead! Genesis 3, after Adam sinned, God literally had to drive Adam out of the Garden and protect the place from him. Likewise, there are people so entrenched in occupying the space in your life and leadership positioning they become detrimental to your ministry that you have to drive them out and protect the space, so they can't come back.

Genesis 3:22-24 (*CEV*), says, "*The Lord said, 'They now know the difference between right and wrong, just as we do. But they must not be allowed to eat fruit from the tree that lets them live forever.' So, the Lord God sent them out of the Garden of Eden, where they would have to work the ground from which the man had been made. Then God put winged creatures at the entrance to the garden and a flaming, flashing sword to guard the way to the life-giving tree.*"

They may not realize it's for their benefit. God did not abandon Adam, He put him in a place where he could deal with him in a more redemptive way. But! Not at the expense of the Garden! The leader must discover the difference between *cost* and *value*. If you, as the leader, fail to recognize and be decisive in assessing the values of other leaders, you may discover too late that you paid more for something of a lesser value. This could put your ministry in position to have to endure a transitional adjustment period. This might also consist of a valuable loss or a casualty of war; so to speak.

During the early years of pastoring, I literally surrounded myself with unqualified leaders who served the purpose of filling a position but lacked one of the three A's (accountability, accessibility, and ability) necessary to proficiently and consistently fulfill the leadership demands of the ministry. It is of no value to have a person in position without the abilities necessary to perform duties required. I often say, *"God never gives a man responsibility without giving him the ability to perform it."* My editor, Carmen, says it this way, *"God doesn't call the equipped, He equips the called!"*

Likewise, it is equally as counter -productive to have a person with abilities who is not accessible. Many organizations are crippled because they attempt to function with an abled-body person whose schedule doesn't allow them to perform in times of service. Probably the most insulting and disloyal of the three A's is a person who has the ability and is accessible, but not accountable, especially during important times and seasons.

The proper use of accountability allows an organization or team to function efficiently, even in the individual's absence. It is the responsibility of this leader to ensure everything they are responsible for is properly completed either by them or a communicating in a timely manner to a superior or peer so that systems and operations continue as required. This allows the individual's accountabilities to be carried out in their absence.

The Characteristics of Wisdom
(Proverbs 8:8, 9, 11-18, 20-30, 32-36, ASV)

The standard of wisdom: "All the words of my mouth are in righteousness; there is nothing crooked or perverse in them. They are all plain to him that understandeth, and right to them that find knowledge."

No comparisions: "For wisdom is better than rubies; And all the things that may be desired are not to be compared unto it. I, Wisdom, have made prudence my dwelling, and find out knowledge and discretion."

Wisdom's adversaries: "The fear of Jehovah is to hate evil: Pride, and arrogancy, and the evil way, And the perverse mouth, do I hate. Counsel is mine, and sound knowledge: I am understanding; I have might."

Wisdom's promotion: "By me kings reign, And princes decree justice. By me princes rule, And nobles, even all the judges of the earth. I love them that love me; And those that seek me diligently shall find me. Riches and honor are with me; Yea, durable wealth and righteousness."

Wisdom's way: "I walk in the way of righteousness, In the midst of the paths of justice; That I may cause those that love me to inherit substance, And that I may fill their treasuries."

God never did anything without it: "Jehovah possessed me in the beginning of his way, Before his works of old. I was set up from everlasting, from the beginning, Before the earth was. When there were no depths, I was brought forth, when there were no fountains abounding with water. Before the mountains were settled, Before the hills was I brought forth; While as yet he had not made the earth, nor the fields, Nor the beginning of the dust of the world.

When he established the heavens, I was there: When he set a circle upon the face of the deep, when he made firm the skies above, When the fountains of the deep became strong, When he gave to the sea its bound, that the waters should not transgress his commandment, When he marked out the foundations of the earth; Then I was by him, as a master workman; And I was daily his delight, Rejoicing always before him."

Wisdom's promise: "Now therefore, my sons, hearken unto me; For blessed are they that keep my ways. Hear instruction, and be wise, And refuse it not. Blessed is the man that heareth me, Watching daily at my gates, Waiting at the posts of my doors. For whoso findeth me findeth life, And shall obtain favor of Jehovah. But he that sinneth against me wrongeth his own soul: All they that hate me love death."

CHAPTER 10
Lessons of Leadership

Nadab and Abihu had no training in the area of self-control or self-discipline in their youth. Aaron's lack of firmness led him to neglect the discipline of his children. This allowed them to develop the habit of self-indulgence which persuaded them to follow their own inclinations, instead of God's order. This is what Paul addresses in Romans 10:1-3, when speaking about their zeal and fervent minds.

Like Aaron's sons, they were never taught to respect the authority of their father and they did not realize the necessity of exact obedience as the requirements of God as Priest. So, they became subjects of *divine judgement*. Isaiah 5:20-24 says God warned by the prophet: "*No leader should deceive himself with the belief that a part of his orders are nonessential, or, that he would accept a substitute for what he has required.*"

> Jeremiah the prophet said, "Who is he that saith
> and it comes to pass, when the Lord did not
> command it?" (Lamentations 3:37)

God has not placed any commands in His Word that any man may disobey at will and not suffer the consequences. To communicate the severity of their offense, Moses said to Aaron and to his sons; Eleazar and Ithamar: *"Do not uncover your heads, nor rend your clothes; lest you die also because the Anointing oil of the Lord is upon you."* And Aaron was silent. Even though it tore at his heart he gave his feelings no expression because God would not allow him to manifest his grief and it be seen as if he sympathized with their sin. This would have caused the congregation to murmur against God.

This example was also the detriment of Uzzah. After David was firmly established on the throne as King, he was led to bring up the Ark of God to Jerusalem. The Ark of God represented the divine presence of God and therefore David decided it should be placed in the capital of the nation; Jerusalem, approximately nine miles from its current location. The Ark of God was brought out from the House of Abinadab and placed upon a new cart pulled by oxen while two of the sons of a Abinadab attended to it.

Over 30,000 of the leading men of Israel followed the Ark with praise and rejoicing all the way to the Holy city. But when they came to Nachon's Threshing floor, Uzzah put forth his hand to the Ark of God and took hold of it, because the oxen shook it. And the anger of the Lord was kindled against Uzzah, and God smote him there for his rashness. And he died right there by the Ark of God, suddenly. David was astonished and greatly disturbed and in his heart he questioned the justice of God. But Moses had given special instruction concerning the transportation of the Ark. No one but the priest, who were the descendants of Aaron could touch it or even to look upon it, while it was uncovered.

The divine direction stipulated, *"...the sons of Kohath shall come to bear it: but they shall not touch any Holy thing, lest they die."* (Numbers 4:15, 7:9)

In this instance, David and his people assembled to perform a sacred work and they had engaged and it seemed good, But the Lord could not accept the service because it was not performed in accordance with His directions. Let's examine an important point. The Scripture reveals that the Philistines, who did not have a knowledge of God's law, had placed the ark upon a cart when they returned it to Israel and the Lord accepted their effort. But, the Israelites had a plain statement of God's will concerning all these matters in their hands and they neglected the instructions which dishonored God.

This means that Uzzah was guilty of the sin of presumption. And by this judgment God designed to impress upon all Israel the importance of giving strict obedience to his requirements. This divine rebuke taught David, as king, to realize the sacredness of the Lord God and the necessity of strict obedience. So, at the end of three months, David decided to make another attempt to remove the Ark but this time, he gave earnest attention to every specific detail. Achan, the descendant of Zerah; son of Judah. Judah was put to death for stealing the devoted spoil in Jericho. He's presented as an example to keep all leaders conscious of the range and impact of rebellious sin. (Joshua chapter 7) A leaders' rebellion can manifest in many unfavorable ways impacting both their personal and family lives.

In Deuteronomy 4:1-6, Moses rehearsed before Israel the wisdom of being instructed in kingdom affairs. "Now, o' Israel, listen to the statutes and the judgments which I teach you to observe, that you may live, and go in and possess the land which the LORD God of your fathers is giving you. You shall not add to the word which I command you, nor take from it, that you may keep the commandments of the LORD your God which I command you. Your eyes have seen what the LORD did at Baal Peor; for the LORD your God has destroyed from among you all the men who followed Baal of Peor. But you who held fast to the LORD your God are alive today, every one of you. 'Surely I have taught you statutes and judgments, just as the LORD my God commanded me, that you should act according to them in the land which you go to possess.'"

How to cover yourself as a leader

Therefore be careful to observe them; for this is your wisdom and your understanding in the sight of the people who will hear all these statutes, and say, 'Surely this great nation is a wise and understanding people.' There are also laws for unintentional and presumptuous sin.

(Numbers 15:22-29, *NKJV*) "You shall have one law for him who sins unintentionally, for him who is native-born among the children of Israel and for the stranger who dwells among them." (15:30-31) "'But the person who does anything presumptuously, whether he is native-born or a stranger, that one brings reproach on the LORD, and he shall be cut off from among his people. Because he has despised the word of the LORD, and has broken His commandment, that person shall be completely cut off; his guilt shall be upon him."

It is important to review Proverbs 29:18, because the kingdom leader need also learn how to correspond with their ministry's vision. Honor ensures that we give to and extract from proper positional graces, human agencies, ordained connections and associations and respect that God requires. But, honor first recognizes the need to discriminate (apply extra caution and special reverence) where *authority* is present or *orders* are given. When you *honor* the natural and spiritual chain of authority you establish a covenant bridge between natural and spiritual blessings.

This is why honor is the active seed for *access:* "The acts of God issued from His throne and His throne is established on His authority. All things were created through God's authority and all physical laws of the universe are maintained by His authority." Hence, the Bible expresses it as *'upholding all things by the word of his power,'* which means upholding all things by the *Word* of the power of *His authority.* For God's authority represents God, Himself, where as His power stands only for His act. Sin against *power* is more easily forgiven than sin against *authority.* Because the latter is a *sin against God, Himself.* God, alone, is *Authority* in all things; all the authorities of the Earth are instituted by God. "Authority is a tremendous thing in the universe. *Nothing* overshadows it. It is therefore *imperative* for us who desire to serve God *to know the authority* of God." (*Spiritual Authority* by Watchman Née)

One of the most quoted and violated principles of the kingdom way and rule is:

"Let all things be done *decently* and in *order.*"
(1 Corinthians 14:40)

The word: *Akeraios*, is a word translated as untainted with what is evil. It is of metal which has no trace of alloy, or of wine or milk undiluted with water. It describes something which is absolutely free from all vices and pure of any corruption. The Christian leader is one whose utter sincerity must be beyond all doubt. To obtain this reference the kingdom leader must be willing to operate consistently under the standards designed to regulate and govern fellowship among God's people.

In the book of Romans 13:1–7, Paul instructs all Believers to be governed and regulated by appointed authority to God's mandate: *"Let every soul be subject to the governing authorities."* For there is no authority except *from* God and the authorities that exist on Earth are appointed *by* God. Therefore, whoever resists the authority resists the ordinance of God. Those who resist will bring judgment on themselves.

Rulers are not a terror to good works, but to evil. Do you want to be unafraid of the authority? "Do what is good and you will have praise from the same. For he is God's minister to you for good. But if you do evil, be afraid; for he does not bear the sword in vain; for he is God's minister, an avenger to execute wrath on him who practices evil. Therefore, be subject, not only because of wrath but also for the sake of your conscience." The Amplified reads, *"Let every soul (person) be loyally subject to the governing (civil) authorities.* For there is no authority except from God [by His permission, His sanction], and those that exist do so by God's appointment." (Proverbs 8:15)

"Therefore, he who resists and sets himself up against the authorities resists what God has appointed and arranged [in divine order]. And those who resist will bring down judgment upon themselves [receiving the penalty due them]. For civil authorities are not a terror to [people of] good conduct, but to [those of] bad behavior. Would you have no dread of him who is in authority? Then do what is right and you will receive his approval and commendation. For he is God's servant for your good. But if you do wrong, [you should dread him and] be afraid, for he does not bear and wear the sword for nothing.

He is God's servant to execute His wrath (punishment, vengeance) on the wrongdoer. Therefore, one must be subject, not only to avoid God's wrath and escape punishment, but also as a matter of principle and for the sake of conscience."

Here, it is clear that everyone is required to render due obedience to those who occupy positions of outstanding authority, simply because there is no authority which is not allotted its place by God. These representative authorities have been set in their places by God. This means that everyone who sets themselves up against authority has really set themselves up against God's arrangement of things: *"Those who do set themselves against authority will receive condemnation upon themselves."*

"Have ye not read even this scripture: The stone which the builders rejected, the same was made the head of the corner" (Mark 12:10, *ASV*) On first read, this passage may appear extremely demanding and flawed to some degree. But, this is a commandment which runs through the entire New Testament. First Timothy 2:1, 2 says, *"I urge that supplications, prayers, intercessions, and thanksgivings should be made for everyone, for kings and for all who are in high positions, so that we may lead a quiet and peaceable life in all godliness and dignity.*" The advice to the leader in Titus 3:1 says: "*Remind them to be subject to rulers and authorities, to be obedient, to be ready for every good work.*"

First Peter 2:13–17: "For the Lord's sake we are to accept the authority of every human institution, whether of the Emperor's as supreme, or of governors, as sent by him to punish those who do wrong and to praise those who do right. For it is God's will that by doing right you should put to silence the ignorance of the foolish."

You cannot be an effective Christian leader if you are undisciplined. The great commission is about exactly that; making disciples. That's what Matthew 28:18, 19 is about: "And Jesus came and spoke to them, saying, 'All authority has been given to Me in heaven and on earth. Go therefore and make disciples of all the nations.'" The mere fact that we have to make disciples implies the need to empower through enlightenment and equip to live a disciplined life, which is, in kingdom citizenship, a regimented walk.

In the Kingdom of God, as we aspire to serve the Lord Jesus Christ, we deny all rights and place our focus on becoming submissive to a new order within the scope of God's Kingdom. The intent in the life of a Christian is that they become submitted to the new order. That *new order* is kingdom dominion mentioned in the Old Testament and is the offspring of the righteousness of God in the New Testament. A lack of order, discipline, and protocol is the primary reason today's Believers may exist without manifestation to confirm their faith, or conform to a productive kingdom lifestyle.

The point I want you to get is, without discipline we cannot properly attain to authority. Now is the time for kingdom order to be restored to the body of Christ, especially in places where true Believers are making a difference. Because we cannot influence the world system without kingdom discipline. Matthew 12:22-30 says, "Then was brought unto him one possessed with a devil, blind, and dumb: and he healed him, insomuch that the blind and dumb both spake and saw. And all the people were amazed, and said, Is not this the son of David? But when the Pharisees heard it, they said, this fellow doth not cast out devils, but by Beelzebub the prince of the devils. And Jesus knew their thoughts, and said unto them, every kingdom divided against itself is brought to desolation; and every city or house divided against itself shall not stand:

And if Satan cast out Satan, he is divided against himself; how shall then his kingdom stand? And if I by Beelzebub cast out devils, by whom do your children cast them out? Therefore they shall be your judges. But if I cast out devils by the Spirit of God, then the kingdom of God is come unto you. Or else how can one enter into a strong man's house, and spoil his goods, except he first bind the strong man? and then he will spoil his house. He that is not with me is against me; and he that gathereth not with me scattereth abroad."

The fact is that as long as we have indiscipline people that do not love the kingdom way enough to commit to its discipline, we will continue to be divided against ourselves and we cannot stand. So if we want to be effective and able to stand so the works of God can go forth, we must pursue a walk of discipline. This is why we pray, study, meditate, fast and give. We praise and worship constantly; all of these things we do to add to a disciplined life. However, this discipline must begin within our *own* thinking!

In Conclusion

When we become a leader thirsty for change, with a hunger and desire to have more of God in our daily lives, there are certain attributes, behaviors, and practices we incorporate into our lives and ministry to become more pleasing to Him. These are the things that set us apart and protect us from the conundrums and chaos of leadership and allows us to operate a ministry of integrity. One that is submissive to God and His ordinances. To you, I say, be thirsty! Be thirsty for more of God in your leadership role, in the operation and growth of your ministry! Thirst for more of Him in *everything* you do, because God, the ultimate leader, will quench your thirst and provide guidance to those who seek Him!

The reprimanded leader

"Israel settled down and remained in Shittim and the people began to play the harlot with the daughters of Moab, who invited the [Israelites] to the sacrifices of their gods, and [they] ate and bowed down to Moab's gods. So Israel joined himself to [the god] Baal of Peor. And the anger of the Lord was kindled against Israel. And the Lord said to Moses, Take all the leaders or chiefs of the people, and hang them before the Lord in the sun [after killing them], that the fierce anger of the Lord may turn away from Israel." (Numbers 25:1-4, *AMP*)

Moses does not receive the promise. "Then I pleaded

with the LORD at that time, saying: 'O Lord GOD, You have begun to show Your servant Your greatness and Your mighty hand, for what god is there in heaven or on earth who can do anything like Your works and Your mighty deeds? I pray, let me cross over and see the good land beyond the Jordan, those pleasant mountains, and Lebanon.' But the LORD was angry with me on your account, and would not listen to me. So the LORD said to me: 'Enough of that! Speak no more to Me of this matter. Go up to the top of Pisgah, and lift your eyes toward the west, the north, the south, and the east; behold it with your eyes, for you shall not cross over this Jordan. But command Joshua, and encourage him and strengthen him; for he shall go over before this people, and he shall cause them to inherit the land which you will see.'"

There are twelve qualifications to identify kingdom leaders along with supporting Scriptures. Those qualifiers are:

1. Able and God-fearing (Exodus 18:21; 2 Samuel 23:3; Ezra 7:25)
2. Be truthful (Exodus 18:21; Deuteronomy 16:19)
3. They should not be covetous (Exodus 18:21)
4. They should have a disposition to refuse bribes (Exodus 23:8)
5. They need to be wise and understanding (Deuteronomy 1:13)
6. Be prominent within the tribes (Deuteronomy 1:13)
7. Must love justice and judgment (Deuteronomy 1:16; 16:18, 19; 27:19; Zechariah 7:9-10)

8. No respecter of persons (Deuteronomy 1:17; 16:19; 25:1; Isaiah 5:23)
9. Be fearless (Deuteronomy 1:17)
10. Conscientious (Deuteronomy 1:17)
11. Strong and courageous (Joshua 1:7)
12. Obedient to the law (Joshua 1:7,8)

There are seven blessings that the nation of Israel would have experienced had they believed Moses as he commanded them and not sent spies to scope out the land and advise if it was as God described. Those blessings are:

1. They would have settled in Canaan forty years earlier.
2. The old generation would not have been condemned to die (Numbers 14)
3. They would have experienced freedom from forty years of hardships, plagues, and other curses. (Numbers 14-25)
4. God would have been honored and glorified by their act of bravery when standing on His Word. (Numbers 13-14)
5. They would not have suffered disgrace or defeat by their enemies (Numbers 14:40-45)
6. Had they not rebelled they may have avoided Kora's death and enjoyed peace and longevity. (Numbers 16-17)
7. They would have experienced better living conditions forty years earlier and the people would have had food and raiment. (Numbers 11:20)

As a leader thirsty for more of God and His blessings, there are seven things to hold true to in order for you to be steadfast among all leaders. Those seven things are:

1. Include all members and keep them involved in your prayers and confessions. This enables you to demonstrate your selfless determination and keep everyone on board so everyone looks good! (Note that historically, many may not expect you to have their best interest at heart.)
2. Strategize effectively, knowing how to utilize your team's position, gifts, influence, resources, and connections to fulfill every assignment.
3. Critique yourself and assume responsibility. The results will be a win-win despite your appearance of weakness or compromise. (This initiates the 'Law of the Buy-in' which says, team members must first believe that you look out for their best interest before they will *"buy-in"* to you or your instructions as their leader.)
4. Keep accurate records for back-up. Refuse to reveal any negative reports to lesser powers for a substantial period. Make sure you have exhausted every scriptural method or principle available before exposing negatives.
5. The position you inherit is not an automatic transmission, but a standard shift. That means you will constantly shift gears as you reach your organizational milestones. Here's how it looks, with every successful accomplishment, "The team did it!" But, with every failure: "I'm responsible." Because at the end of the day, it is the leader's responsibility to develop the skills to lead and equip the team for goal accomplishment and task completion.
6. *You* must not allow indifferences to stand in the way of

properly and fairly assessing the talents God has directed to join your stead. Work diligently, stay optimistic, and allow all persons regardless of their historical, nationality, classification, or ethnic backgrounds to dictate their ability to serve. Care for them as if they were your own. Lower every shield or suspicion and foster ways to get closer to *all team members*. Keep this piece of advice in mind: Leaders who focus and operate soley from their past may forfeit their future. However, those who operate by faith focuses on their future, forgetting their past! (Romans 14:23)

7. Your first assignment is not an indictment of your paper skills, but *people* skills. I'm excited for you because I believe *you* have the grace to expand the kingdom!

The twelve 'be-habits' of leaders thirsty for change

1. *Be punctual.* Leaders thirsty for the high call must practice being on time, qualified for service, and answerable. He or she must be strictly observant of appointed times; avoid lateness, strive to be prompt at all costs. This should include appointments, payments, services, spousal dates, time with children and other family members, and socially.

2. *Be positional.* Be in place, dependable, responsible, a weight bearer, always ready to represent. Stay mentally conditioned with reference to place, location, and situations. Be prepared to bargain from a position of

strength, position yourself in a manner of being placed, disposed, and/or arranged: Have the relative posture and mental attitude to stand strong on controversial topics. Hold your position!

3. *Be prepared and ready to serve.* Be ready to serve; stay armed for duty properly expectant, organized, and equipped; steadfast and prepared for hurricanes. Prepared and ready to serve means that you require little or no further preparation to tackle any assignment or situation.

4. *Be focused.* This means you are dissolved of any distractions, conscious mentally. You are a central point of attraction, attention, and activity.

5. *Be delivered.* Free from vice or bias. Be loyal, faithful to one's sovereign, government, or state: be a loyal subject. Remain faithful to your oath, commitments, and obligations. Be loyal to your vows remembering that whatsoever your vow with your mouth is a vow to God. (Deuteronomy 23:23) You must be faithful to any leader, party, or cause, or to any person or thing conceived as deserving fidelity: a loyal friend. Characterized by or showing faithfulness to commitments, vows, allegiance, obligations, etc.: you must be a loyal conduit.

6. *Be vision compliant.* Be flexible and functional. A historian once said, "Any people whose leaders fail to comply with a specific vision will be as those who are idle and play as the scholars do when their master is absent. They do nothing of any good purpose, but stand

all day idle, and sport themselves in the market-place, for want of instruction, what to do and how to do it. These people are scattered as sheep having no shepherd, for want of the masters of assemblies to call them and keep them together." (Mark 6:34) To be flexible and functional requires a detailed understanding of the vision and missions of the ministry so not unanticipated occurrence can offset or detour primary leaders who thirst for change.

7. *Be communicative and competently connected.* Often in ministry, a great deal of confusion arises because leaders who are required to communicate frequently lack the competence necessary to convey detailed information. This usually happens among leaders who boast themselves in measures they are not qualified to perform. Competence requires a suitable or sufficient skill, knowledge, and experience to accomplish specific purposes properly. Positions that demand high volumes of communication and interaction among leaders also demands an all around leader who can adjust swiftly, both in crisis and under pressure. I have personally observed unqualified leaders who sometimes experience anxiety and stressful fears. Sometimes this happens because certain tasks may unmask their inability to function at the level required. And their responses seems to never match their resumes. When leaders are able to competently communicate with all essential personnel,

the organization is immediately impacted in a positive way without personal distractions.

In Acts 15:36-41, Paul was affected by the incompetence of Mark. Then, after some days Paul said to Barnabas, *"Let us now go back and visit our brethren in every city where we have preached the word of the Lord and see how they are doing."* Now Barnabas was determined to take with them, John called Mark. But Paul insisted that they should not take with them the one who had departed from them in Pamphylia and had not gone with them to the work.

Then the contention became so sharp that they parted from one another. And so Barnabas took Mark and sailed to Cyprus; but Paul chose Silas and departed, being commended by the brethren to the grace of God. And he went through Syria and Cilicia, strengthening the churches. Competence among elders, directors, deacons, and all high-ranking leaders is a huge deal. This is why communication must be clear, concise, and confirmable at all times among leaders and followers.

8. *Be steadfast:* Fixed in direction, firm in purpose. Ultimately, this kingdom leader is strong in resolution, full of faith, unshakable, unwavering, adherence, single-minded, faithful, immovable and intensely reliable, relentless and highly trustworthy.

9. *Be reverently honorable.* In object six I stated that a leader always respects authority, both delegated and representative because honor first recognizes the need

to discriminate or demonstrate extra caution /special reverence where authority is present or orders are given. Your decision to honor the natural and spiritual chain of authority is the bridge to covenant natural and spiritual blessings. Honor is the seed for access.

10. *Be submissive.* Inclined or disposed to acquiesce or consent silently. Unresistingly or humbly obedient as a submissive servant. One who is swiftly compliant.

11. *Be diligent.* Constant in effort to accomplish something; attentive to details and persistent in doing anything: always a student of the assignment, done or pursued with persevering attention. Painstaking: a diligent search and researcher.

12. *Be obedient.* Adhere to all of the *'be-habits'* of effective kingdom leaders.

"So then, my beloved brethren, let every man be swift to hear, slow to speak, slow to wrath; for the wrath of man does not produce the righteousness of God. Therefore, lay aside all filthiness and overflow of wickedness, and receive with meekness the implanted word, which is able to save your souls. But be doers of the word, and not hearers only, deceiving yourselves. For if anyone is a hearer of the word and not a doer, he is like a man observing his natural face in a mirror; for he observes himself, goes away, and immediately forgets what kind of man he was. But he who looks into the perfect law of liberty and continues in it, and is not a forgetful hearer but a doer of the work, this one will be blessed in what he does. If anyone among you thinks he is religious, and does not bridle his tongue but deceives his own heart, this one's religion is useless. Pure and undefiled religion before God and the Father is this: to visit orphans and widows in their trouble, and to keep oneself unspotted from the world. (James 1:19-27, *NKJV*)

You Must Expect transitional adjustments to become frequent demands relative to your leadership position in the kingdom. Progress in knowledge continually because the assignment is spiritual and requires continual growth and intentional mind renewal. There is a peril in *not progressing.*

In closing, review what the Word in Hebrews 6:1-20 says:

"Therefore, leaving the discussion of the elementary principles of Christ, let us go on to perfection, not laying again the foundation of repentance from dead works and of faith toward God. Of the doctrine of baptisms, of laying on of hands, of resurrection of the dead, and of eternal judgment. And this we will do if God permits."

May God's blessings saturate your life; your good works, your ministry, staff, family, and all that your hands shall touch. May He elevate your call, your ministry, your staff, and birth many new leaders under your stead. As you thirst for His continued guidance, may His anointing satisfy, edify, and rectify your ministry to new levels in Christ our Lord; Amen.

www.ingramcontent.com/pod-product-compliance
Lightning Source LLC
Chambersburg PA
CBHW072012090426
42740CB00011B/2168